HOPELESS AROMANTIC

of related interest

Ace Voices
What it Means to Be Asexual, Aromantic, Demi or Grey-Ace
Eris Young
ISBN 978 1 78775 698 4
eISBN 978 1 78775 699 1

Amazing Ace, Awesome Aro
An Illustrated Exploration
Victoria Barron
ISBN 978 1 83997 714 5
eISBN 978 1 83997 715 2

Sounds Fake But Okay
An Asexual and Aromantic Perspective on Love,
Relationships, Sex, and Pretty Much Anything Else
Sarah Costello and Kayla Kaszyca
ISBN 978 1 83997 001 6
eISBN 978 1 83997 002 3

HOPELESS AROMANTIC

An Affirmative Guide to Aromanticism

Samantha Rendle

Foreword by Sarah Costello

Jessica Kingsley Publishers
London and Philadelphia

First published in Great Britain in 2023 by Jessica Kingsley Publishers
An imprint of John Murray Press

I

Copyright © Samantha Rendle 2023

Foreword Copyright © Sarah Costello 2023

Content Warning: This book includes references to sexual
abuse, depression, anxiety and self-harm.

A CIP catalogue record for this title is available from the
British Library and the Library of Congress

ISBN 978 1 83997 367 3
eISBN 978 1 83997 368 0

Printed and bound in the United States by Integrated Books International

Jessica Kingsley Publishers' policy is to use papers that are natural,
renewable and recyclable products and made from wood grown in
sustainable forests. The logging and manufacturing processes are expected
to conform to the environmental regulations of the country of origin.

Jessica Kingsley Publishers
Carmelite House
50 Victoria Embankment
London EC4Y 0DZ

www.jkp.com

John Murray Press
Part of Hodder & Stoughton Limited
An Hachette UK Company

Contents

Foreword

Any person who identifies on the asexual spectrum is all too familiar with feeling invisible. Feeling ignored, shunned and woefully misunderstood by our broader social order is just baked into the experience. Historically excluded and ostracized from straight and queer communities alike, those who identify under the asexual umbrella of identities have long struggled for acceptance, representation and public legitimacy.

And this is all well and good – (bad, actually, but you get it) – but there is one small problem which you, dear reader, may have already aptly noticed:

The title of the book you are about to read is not *Hopeless Asexual*. It's *Hopeless Aromantic*.

So why start with asexuality? Well, these two identities – asexual and aromantic – are nearly always linked. Or more specifically, aromanticism is linked to asexuality. Not just as it pertains to people like me, who are both aro and ace, but to anyone on the aromantic spectrum. And therein lies the problem.

At best, this inextricable association manifests as an inno-cent ignorance of the concept of the Split Attraction Model, where someone (falsely) believes that asexuality and aromanticism must always be two halves of the same whole. At best, people simply don't understand that romantic and sexual attraction are discrete concepts – that while some people's lived experiences leave them struggling to see any difference between them at all, others can draw a very distinct line between their experiences with the two.

But at worst, the linking of aro and ace identities manifests as a demotion of aromanticism to a mere subset of asexuality – apparently not deserving of its own spaces, conversations and communities. At worst, aromanticism is a second-class citizen, pushed to the side as an afterthought (if it is even thought of at all).

In fact, many conversations around asexuality – especially when directed at or in concert with allosexuals – revolve around assuring allos that asexuals can still experience romantic attraction, can still date and have lasting romantic relationships, can still be *normal like you*. 'Don't be afraid of us', some asexuals overtly imply, 'at least we're not heartless.' They keep that romantic attraction in their back pockets, ready to wield as a weapon at the drop of a hat, as if it's evidence that they are still human.

This book, on the other hand, is for those who are still profoundly and often painfully human, but whose back pockets come up empty. Those whose pockets contain *something*, but it's locked in a box and they can't even get it open, much less decipher what it is. Those whose pockets have holes, and sometimes the contents just slip out and disappear without warning. Those whose pockets – okay, you get it. This metaphor is getting out of hand.

The point is, aromanticism is often overshadowed by the almighty asexuality. Which is funny in a sad, sick sort of way, because even today, after decades of valiant effort, activism and community-building, asexuality remains only on the outskirts of public discourse around queerness and queer living. And if asexual representation and visibility remain woefully inadequate, the situation is even more dire for the aro-specs among us. When a growing community such as ours still lacks a robust patchwork of well-informed support systems, every conversation matters.

I'm not sure Sam would call herself an arospec elder – people are so rarely inclined to give themselves such a title, especially when they're only 29, and especially when in recent years their labels have changed continuously until they ultimately chose to forgo labels altogether. But as I read through this very book, I couldn't help but think of Sam as a friendly elder taking my hand and guiding me through its pages.

Traditionally, we expect our community 'elders' to be firm in their identities and unchanging in their understanding of themselves; but if the A identities teach us anything, it is that identity is fluid. It can transform and mould to each version of ourselves, at each age as the years pass, whether we wish for a stack of specific labels that describe our every experience, or whether even the broadness of the word 'queer' feels too specific for our taste.

So if anything, Sam's evolution, that open admission of ongoing questioning even while writing this book, makes her perspective only that much more valuable.

As much as Sam may question her place in the aro community, the stories and guidance of folks like her – who, like so many others, are not inextricably cemented into their identity – prove indispensable for anyone looking to wade deeper into the world of aromanticism.

So go forth, dear reader, and let Sam lead you into the

aromantic promised land. Whether you're a baby aro, a more weathered one or an ally with a curiosity about our community, there is always something new to discover.

Sarah Costello, co-author of *Sounds Fake But Okay: An Asexual and Aromantic Perspective on Love, Relationships, Sex, and Pretty Much Anything Else*

Introduction

Hi, friends! My name is Sam, and for a period of time in my life I identified as aromantic asexual. I've since changed my label to aroaceflux (but that's a bit of a mouthful for the opening sentence), and at present my label is just a big question mark. And that's okay. I'll get into that later.

In short, aromantic asexual means you experience little to no romantic or sexual attraction. I discovered the term in the summer of 2018 when I terminated a fleeting Tinder courtship having panicked about the guy being absolutely perfect but somehow failing to stir the butterflies inside me.

I remember that night perfectly: I was cleaning my teeth with my sister, getting ready for bed, and we were talking about a man I'd been on a couple of dates with. On paper, he was perfect for me: he was a vegetarian, he had an amazing sense of humour, he liked all the things I liked and he was absolutely gorgeous. But something still felt wrong. I felt anxious about seeing him, and I was frankly terrified of being intimate with him. I told my sister all of this that night, and we were discussing it in great detail before I blurted, 'I'd say I'm asexual, but I'm pretty sure that means you fancy yourself.' First of all, for all the asexual people reading this, I'm slapping my forehead along with you. But as stupid as that sentence was, it's a sentence that changed my life, because the next day I looked up 'asexual' on the internet and I found a video called 'AROMANTIC ASEXUAL: Q&A', which basically put into words how I'd been feeling for most of my life. The video has since been removed due to controversy surrounding the creator;[1] luckily, I took many, many notes from it and can share with you a few quotes that struck a chord with me:

'I've been aesthetically attracted to people – I thought they were nice-looking.'

'I've always been distant when it came to romance and lacked that interest.'

'I always thought there was something wrong with me.'

I cannot describe to you how relieved and *seen* I felt having watched that and countless other videos by other creators. Discovering that there was terminology to describe how I felt was so exciting to me, and it took me no time at all to bombard my YouTube subscribers with news of my shiny new labels, throw money at a vendor for a flag at my first ever Pride parade and come out to my mum for the millionth time (it took a lot of experimenting to discover myself, let me tell you). I took *so much pride* in my identity.

Prior to my monumental discovery, I'd read the term

---

1 I'm unaware of what actually happened and am not affiliated with/do not support this creator. However, it cannot be denied that the video I saw that day helped me discover aromanticism.

'asexual' in a book somewhere. The term was barely brushed upon in a teen romance novel if I remember correctly, but it obviously stuck in my subconscious for a reason. I didn't learn the term 'aromantic' until I watched the video mentioned above, but I do wonder if I'd have found my labels had it not been for that fleeting mention of asexuality in a book I barely remember.

Looking back as far as my secondary school days (I was probably somewhere between 14 and 16), I can recall the band members I 'fancied' – boys with swoopy black fringes and thick eyeliner – but I realize now that I didn't actually *fancy* them. In my teenage fantasies, I was never having sex with them; I was never kissing them or even holding their hand. I just liked how they looked and what they could do. The only time I ever pictured them in romantic situations was with each other (don't look at me like that – I know you've shipped people, too[2]). I told my friends that I fancied these beautiful emo boys because that's what I was *supposed* to do. Turns out it was pretty much just hero worship.

Unfortunately, not everyone who discovers they lack some level of attraction to people will be happy about it. I see a lot of people on my Twitter feed lamenting about being forever alone, and I get it. Being a minority in this world is hard, but being a minority that *no one knows about* is something else entirely. If asexuality is barely known, aromanticism might as well be a myth. It's *not* a myth, but very few people know about it, and that can make aromantic people feel small. Even as I came to grips with my labels, I promoted asexuality far more than I promoted aromanticism, and that was probably

. . . .

2   Shipping is defined as hoping or believing two people are in a relationship.

because more people knew what it was – or had at least heard of it – and that meant more engagement. It's not something I'm proud of, but I'm here to change that.

A 2014 study involving over 14,000 people estimated that 1% of the human population is asexual, and 25.9% of those people are aromantic. The same study found that 4.3% of the 3300 non-asexuals who participated identified as aromantic.[3] Another study, though smaller, found that almost 1% of its participants were aromantic.[4] If we average out those three percentages, we come to 1.85%, which is a *very* rough number since it is only based it on two small studies, but if you imagine that number to be close to accurate, that means there could potentially be 140.6 million aromantics among us. That's a *lot* of people feeling under-represented. That's a lot of people worrying that they'll face an abyss of eternal loneliness because they don't feel romantic attraction.

Here's the good news: romantic orientation is only one of many orientations. Most people's orientations line up, meaning they're romantically and sexually attracted to the same group of genders – someone who is homosexual is both sexually and romantically attracted to the same gender – but some people's don't. So just because you might not feel romantic attraction, it does not mean you can't experience love or other types of attraction. Deep love can be experienced through friendships or familial relationships. You could even

3   Ace Community Survey (2014) 'Cross-orientations among non-aces.' Accessed on 3/11/2022 at https://acecommunitysurvey.org/2014/11/17/cross-orientations-among-non-aces

4   Lund, E.M., Thomas, K.B., Sias, C.M. and Bradley, A.R. (2016) 'Examining concordant and discordant sexual and romantic attraction in American adults: Implications for Counselors.' *Journal of LGBT Issues in Counseling 10*, 4, 211–226.

find a non-romantic life partner (more on that later). Some aromantic people even manage to find romantic love against the odds. Aromanticism doesn't always mean you *completely* lack romantic attraction; some aromantic people feel a degree of it.

I personally am still unsure where on the aromantic spectrum I fit. I know I'm capable of romantic love, and I know I've felt romantic attraction before, but I don't feel it as frequently as a lot of other people do. I meet new people and I often think something along the lines of 'Wow, they're beautiful' or 'They're such a lovely person', but it very rarely goes beyond that. In my 29 years of life, I have experienced romantic attraction four times at varying degrees, and honestly – because I've felt it so infrequently, and often with such low intensity – it's *scary*. A lot of people would suggest that I'm therefore not aromantic, but aromanticism is a *spectrum*.

For most of my life, I've searched for a label that fits me best. I've been in relationships with men and women, and with each relationship I've questioned what that made me and ultimately discovered more about myself. I'm still discovering myself, and orientations can be fluid, so I always have to remind myself that exploring and questioning is okay. It's okay for you, too.

Reminder: aromanticism is feeling *little* to no romantic attraction. You can still feel a degree of romantic attraction as an aromantic, or it can happen under certain circumstances. If you feel that it fits you as a label, congratulations, and welcome to the community.

So if you're a hopeless aromantic with long-term depression stemming from the fear that you'll be forever alone, or if you're a fresh little aromantic completely new to your orientation and happy to have found your people, or if you're simply questioning or keen to better know your aromantic neighbour, this book is for you. These pages contain advice on coping with loneliness and stigma, finding community and so much more.

Remember, there *might* be 140.6 million aromantics out there. I put very little energy into calculating that number and it's probably not at all accurate, so don't quote me on it, but I'm just saying... There *might* be. So right off the bat, I hope I've made you feel less alone. If not, read on, friend...

CHAPTER 1

Understanding Aromanticism

'Are aromantic and asexual the same thing?'
The second most-searched question on
Google regarding aromanticism ·

Aromanticism is the subject of very little research and is often mistaken for asexuality – an orientation arguably similar to aromanticism that's also under-represented *but* has its own Wikipedia article. Wikipedia reserved a generous *four paragraphs* for aromanticism at the very bottom of its article on romantic orientation.[1] Thanks, Wikipedia. Google Scholar doesn't even recognize aromanticism as a word; type it in, and Scholar spits out numerous pages on romanticism, arguably the opposite of what I looked up. I clicked through 25 pages of Scholar articles, and only two links referenced aromanticism.

So in the wake of the internet's frugality, consider this

· · · · · · · · · · · · · · · ·

1   Wikipedia (2022) 'Romantic orientation.' Accessed on 3/11/2022 at https://en.wikipedia.org/wiki/Romantic_orientation

chapter aromanticism's unofficial Wikipedia article – 'unofficial' being the operative word here because we've all seen how terrible I am at maths, and Wikipedia might come for me if I called it 'official'. I'm not much better at history, but I've scraped together a brief history of aromanticism for your benefit. You can thank me by recommending this book to all your friends.

I'll say it again for the sake of this title's chapter: aromanticism means experiencing *little to no* romantic attraction. The word originates from the Greek prefix a-, meaning 'not' or 'without', which is often used for negation; I'll assume you know what the 'romantic' in 'aromantic' is all about. In the community, 'aromantic' is often shortened to 'aro'. It's up to you how you pronounce it; I personally pronounce it like the pointy thing you shoot from a bow ('arrow' if you're not in the mood for guessing games), but I know some aromantic people pronounce it 'ay-ro' which, okay, makes a bit more sense than my pronunciation, but it's up to the individual.

A brief history

As far as anyone knows, the term 'aromantic' was originally coined on an AVEN[2] forum in 2005. That was only 17 years ago as I write this, and I guarantee aromanticism was a thing for longer than that because I identified as aromantic for a long time and I'm 29. How's that for maths?

AUREA, the Aromantic-spectrum Union for Recognition, Education and Advocacy, is a website that was launched in

2   AVEN (Asexual Visibility and Education Network) is an internet-based community for asexual people: www.asexuality.org

2019 with the aim to educate on aromanticism and provide a community for aromantic people. Their website conveniently has a blog post dedicated to aromantic history, which I encourage you to read, but there's a part I found rather interesting that I'll summarize below.[3]

Sometime in the 1640s, there was a group of women in Guangdong, China, called the Golden Orchid Society, a sisterhood opposed to marriage. Some of these women wore their hair in the same style married women typically did to symbolize their romantic unavailability. Some of them married each other – presumably to avoid being made to marry a man they didn't want to marry – and some entered marriage but refused to consummate.[4] They were so committed to their society and their beliefs that they even took their own lives in protest if one of their members was forced into marriage. Obviously, this was *way* before 2005, so the term 'aromantic' didn't exist, but that sounds pretty darn aromantic to me.

I also took it upon myself to research 'single historical figures', just to see what would come up, and it turns out some pretty big names never married. Jane Austen was one that shocked me; she wrote numerous stories about love but rejected several long-term romantic relationships. It's unclear why she never took anyone up on these proposals, but it did strike a chord with me that she picked romance as her genre but never seemed to crave it herself – for a long time that was me. Romance has always been one of my favourite things to write about, whether I've been in a romantic relationship or

3 AUREA (2019) 'Aromantic history.' Accessed on 3/11/2022 at www.aromanticism.org/en/news-feed/aromantic-history
4 Wikipedia (2021) 'Golden Orchid Society.' Accessed on 3/11/2022 at https://en.wikipedia.org/wiki/Golden_Orchid_Society

completely repulsed by the idea, and it's interesting to think that Jane Austen could've been in the same boat. Perhaps she and I shared a fascination with things we didn't have or didn't fully understand the nuances of. We'll never know, alas, because her sister burned most of their correspondence after Jane's death, so the juicy gossip is nothing but dust now.

Another historical figure who never married was Leonardo da Vinci. This one is just as tricky because although it was unclear if he ever engaged in sexual or romantic relationships with anyone of any gender, it *was* rumoured that he dabbled in a spot of sodomy. Maybe he did – it's really not my business – but sex does not always equal romance. There's much speculation about him being gay, but maybe he was both gay *and* aromantic? Remember earlier in the book when I said your orientations don't always line up? This is a perfect example (though unconfirmed): Leonardo could've been *sexually* attracted to men (homosexual) but *romantically* attracted to no one (aromantic). It's another mystery we'll never solve, but there's an entire Wikipedia article dedicated entirely to his personal life, separate from his main article,[5] where I found a quote that sounded rather aromantic:[6]

> Whoso curbs not lustful desires puts himself on a level with the beasts.

Other examples of single historical figures include Sir Isaac Newton, who was rumoured to have died a virgin, and Florence

---

5   Thanks, Wikipedia, for giving Leonardo *two whole articles*, but aromanticism four puny paragraphs!

6   Wikipedia (2022) 'Personal life of Leonardo da Vinci.' Accessed on 3/11/2022 at https://en.wikipedia.org/wiki/Personal_life_of_Leonardo_da_Vinci#Sexuality

Nightingale, who seemed to lack any interest whatsoever in companionship. Florence Nightingale was extremely career-driven, mind you, so maybe she just didn't have the time or patience for a relationship – *or* maybe she was just a bit aromantic.

Of course, just because someone is single, it doesn't necessarily mean it's because they lack some sort of attraction. There are many reasons why someone might choose to be single, but it's interesting to speculate.

SAM

Unfortunately, this section isn't all about me, Sam, but SAM, the Split Attraction Model. SAM suggests that there are several types of attraction (sensual, platonic, romantic and sexual being a few) and that they don't always coincide (as with the above example of Leonardo da Vinci). If you identify as gay or straight, SAM probably isn't all that useful for you, but for other people it can be a useful tool to put a label on how they're feeling about people.

Here's a quick guide to the above types of attraction:

- Sensual – the desire to be touched by someone in a way that isn't inherently sexual (e.g. hugging or cuddling).
- Platonic – the desire to be friends with someone.
- Romantic – the desire to pursue a romantic relationship with someone.
- Sexual – the desire to perform sexual acts with someone.

These aren't all the types of attraction, but they're the basic ones. Others include alterous, emotional and intellectual attraction.

As I said, for a lot of people these attractions line up. But some people feel romantic attraction to one group of people but are sexually attracted to another. Some people might be biromantic heterosexual (romantically attracted to multiple genders, but sexually attracted only to one gender). Some aromantic people identify as asexual as well, meaning their attractions line up, but many aromantic people do feel sexual attraction.

According to LGBTQIA+ Wiki,[7] split attraction was first explored in the works of German writer and homosexual pioneer Karl Heinrich Ulrichs in 1879, but only in 2005 did the Split Attraction Model commonly cited by the A communities (that's asexual, aromantic and agender people) begin to form, and it was another four years before the term was common knowledge in our communities.

The Split Attraction Model can be a useful tool for discovering your identity. Many people in the A communities have historically struggled with knowing what labels to use because most of us had never heard these terms before. It could be beneficial to anyone questioning their identity to really sit down with these terms and ask themselves what sort of attraction they may be feeling towards particular people. Are you sexually attracted to people of the same gender as you but don't want the romantic attachment? Perhaps you could be aromantic and homosexual. Is the crush you're experiencing *super intense* but not romantic or sexual? Perhaps you're feeling platonic attraction.

If you are reading this and struggling with your feelings, I encourage you to really sit with the types of attraction listed

7   LGBTQIA+ Wiki (n.d.) 'Split Attraction Model.' Accessed on 3/11/2022 at https://lgbtqia.fandom.com/wiki/Split_Attraction_Model

above. Make a list of your friends and loved ones and try to work out which types of attraction you feel towards each person. Look up other types of attraction as well. You might find someone painfully pleasing to look at, but it might not go beyond that. Ask yourself: do I just want to look at this person because of their amazing bone structure, or do I also want to put my mouth on that bone structure? What sort of attraction am I feeling towards this person? Can I put a label on that?

But it's equally important to note that not everyone needs labels, and that's fine, too. At the time of writing this particular chapter, I can confidently say I'm feeling all of those types of attraction, which is confusing to a person who considered herself aromantic for a long time, but I'm trying to be okay with putting my labels aside for now.

The aromantic spectrum

As I mentioned in the Introduction, aromanticism is a spectrum. On one end of the spectrum is feeling romantic attraction (alloromanticism), and on the other is feeling no romantic attraction (aromanticism). However, it's not necessarily a straight line. Some aromantic people fluctuate across the spectrum, occasionally feeling a degree of romantic attraction and feeling no romantic attraction the rest of the time. Some aromantic people feel romantic attraction only when a bond has been formed (this is called demiromanticism).

Being such an unrecognized orientation, aromanticism faces plenty of misconceptions. *How I Met Your Mother*'s Barney Stinson is often used as an example of an aromantic person: he's for the most part uninterested in commitment, cold and mean-spirited. Later on in the show, he does embark on romantic ventures, but that doesn't mean to say he still can't fall on the aromantic spectrum. This isn't confirmed in the show, and it isn't a *completely* flattering example for our community, but Barney Stinson is a semi-realistic character with flaws and strengths who's generally well liked. Although a common misconception is that every aromantic person is a promiscuous white man like Barney, aromantic people do in fact belong to different gender identities, sexual orientations, races, religious groups and other demographics – and they're not all cold and mean-spirited like Barney! *There isn't one way to be aromantic.*

I've explored a couple of labels on the aromantic spectrum and sometimes I still question where exactly I fit, or if I fit at all any more. Since I started writing this book, I've had a very inconveniently timed personal crisis. I entered into a romantic relationship as I was signing the contract for this book, and having already started typing it, I had to make a few changes. I have no doubt I'm going to have to make more changes before I finish because my emotions are chaotic, and my relationship status is all over the place. Here's what I wrote before the brief relationship ended:

As an aromantic spectrum (or aro-spec for short) person in a romantic relationship, it's very difficult to explain to other people why I feel I still identify with this label. Upon first discovering the label, I felt fully aromantic – no desire to be in a relationship, and no attraction to match – but in the three years since discovering my orientation I've realized it's not completely right for me. You could argue that I'm more demiromantic because I knew my partner for almost two years before we got together and we developed a strong bond long before even meeting in person. I've been identifying as aro-flux (a label for someone who fluctuates on the aromantic spectrum) for a while, which could also fit. I'm comfortable with either, because if for some reason my relationship were to end, I know the chances of me building up that attraction with someone else are slim. I usually just use 'aromantic' or 'aro-spec' because it's easier, and, to be honest, I don't really owe anyone but my partner any further explanation.

Some of the above is still true, especially the part about owing no one an explanation. I feel it's important to keep the things I wrote in the book despite no longer being with this person because, as I said before, aromanticism is different for everyone, and for me it presents itself differently with any partners I might have.

I actually saved a comment posted on one of my YouTube videos recently because it really struck a chord with me:

I like long-term monogamous relationships which is why I've always connected with demisexuality. But outside of those two relationships [I've been in] I have rarely experienced attraction towards others whatsoever. When I'm single I will have a sex drive and no one I want to have sex with or I long for a romantic situation [with no one in particular in mind], and I have no idea when I will get that opportunity again. It could be a week until I perceive someone as attractive or it could be a year.

This was a comment on one of my videos about being aroflux, and I felt that it explained some of my feelings perfectly. I also feel it explains the difference between libido and attraction very well – libido is your sex drive, and attraction is who it's directed towards. Of course, this book focuses on romantic orientation, but the premise is the same: you can long for a romantic relationship, but the *attraction* isn't always there. Just because aromantic people might not feel attraction, it doesn't mean some of them don't *want* a romantic relationship.

When it comes to physical intimacy, aromantic people all have different preferences. Just because the attraction isn't always there, it doesn't mean some of us don't like kissing or holding hands. Of course, there are plenty of aromantic people who are completely repulsed by any kind of romantic interaction, but there are some who still seek out those kinds of relationships, and it's important to note that however someone feels about physical affection, they can still identify as aromantic.

Was I born this way?

There is much debate, not only regarding aromantic people but people across all three A communities, about whether we were born this way, or if something caused us to be this way. This debate is a sensitive topic in our community – you wouldn't ask a straight person if something happened in their past that resulted in them only being attracted to the opposite gender, so all most aromantics ask is that you show the same respect for them.

I, like many other people, have experienced romance-based trauma in my life, but in spite of not then knowing the term, I was definitely aro-spec prior to those experiences. Nothing that happened to me in my past caused me to change my orientation. I may fluctuate or tweak my labels, but that has everything to do with me and nothing to do with anything else. Orientation is not a choice.

However, I've had many comments on a video I made about trauma-induced orientation from people who *do* identify a certain way because of past experiences, which is also completely valid. Born this way or made this way, however you choose to identify deserves respect and isn't up to anyone else.

I actually looked at the most frequently asked questions regarding aromanticism on Google, and one of them was 'Can you choose to be aromantic?' I repeat: *orientation is not a choice.* Unfortunately, there are many posts online along the lines of 'How do I stop being aromantic?' and 'I hate being aromantic; I don't know how to cope', which is extremely sad, but whether you're happy about your orientation or not, it's not something you can control, and there are ways to thrive and be happy without having to change who you are. This book contains many of those methods.

I still don't get it...

Aromanticism is arguably one of the most complex orientations out there, mainly due to stigma (especially regarding disabled and neurodivergent aros) and lack of knowledge surrounding the topic. Unless you've identified as aro-spec, it's almost impossible to explain and difficult to grasp. In short, it means the person feels limited romantic attraction. That's it. That's the book. Thanks for reading.

Kidding!

Due to the complexities of aromanticism as an orientation, I'd understand if you've read up to this point and still feel unsure if you fall on the aromantic spectrum. The spectrum is broad, encompassing around 16 micro labels,[8] so if you're still unsure, don't worry. Aromanticism is complex enough to…well, fill a book with.

If you still don't understand it yet, that's okay; most people I talk to about aromanticism never fully *get it*. The next chapter is a deep dive into a number of micro labels under the aromantic umbrella; hopefully with all the types broken down, you'll get a better understanding and maybe even find your own label if that's something you want.

The important thing to remember is that labels don't have to be permanent, and you're the only one who can say who you are.

8   Aromantics Wiki (n.d.) 'Romantic orientations.' Accessed on 3/11/2022 at https://aromantic.wikia.org/wiki/Category:Romantic_Orientations

To Be Aromantic

by Ezra John, LGBT+ writer, author of To Be A Trans Man: Our Stories of Transition, Acceptance and Joy

I'm not a confrontational person. I never have been. I'm not selfless by any means, but many of my decisions can be influenced by what I think would make a situation easier to navigate. Much like an elaborate dance, social interaction can have a series of steps that need to be learned. They don't come completely naturally to me, but I always thought that there were certain things that just had to be done. Life is more about making things simpler than anything else. There's nothing simpler than following the rules.

I consider this, and remember an argument with the boyfriend I had during my time at university. I crossed my arms over my chest, self-conscious, and my fingers worried at the skin on my neck. Our kitchen was long, with red terracotta-style tiles, and impeccably clean. He hated it when it got messy. The house was named Linda, and none of her walls were straight. You could see how crooked she was when you looked at the stairs, slanting one way and then the other as you rounded the corner to the top. One of the beams holding up the railing on the landing had been snapped during a party and jammed back into place, splintering at an angle.

'You just don't seem to want to hold my hand', he said. *I don't, I don't, I don't.*

'You don't want to touch me.'

'I do', I replied. It tasted like truth, I thought. Sour. Whatever truth feels like, it has spent too long festering inside me. The words come out so rotten I can't tell the difference. He looks at me for a long time, accusingly.

'I need you to be affectionate. I need to feel like you want to be around me.'

We lie together, and I hate the way his skin feels pressed next to mine. I hate the sweat sticking his arm to the small of my back. Does anyone actually enjoy spooning? I begin to think it's a myth perpetuated deliberately to make my life miserable. Our legs tangle in the sheets, and I imagine documentary footage of a spider wrapping up a fly. I tell him I'll try harder and I'm sorry and I love him. Two truths and a lie.

It took a long time to extricate myself from the difference between love and shame. To consider life as something other than a series of scripted events. Other people were not, in fact, waiting for me to take their cues. People were supposed to want to fall in love, but what did I want? What do I want? Eventually, obviously, he and I fell apart. Sitting in a café as I explained what I could not do, and then sitting in the kitchen feeling guilty for it anyway, I made him feel unwanted. Like he wasn't good enough.

I thought he was my best friend.

When you go through your entire life existing in your body, it's difficult to figure out that there's some great experience that you are, for some reason, not partial to. Especially something as difficult to define as romantic attraction. It's the universal constant. Our single human experience. Why would anyone feel the need to explain it? I was left with the films and the songs, and the assumption that one day things would all fall into place, and I would suddenly understand everything. Until then, they were probably exaggerating. I had been a bit sad when relationships ended, but reduced to tears seemed a touch excessive. A bruised ego was painful, perhaps, but it wasn't that different from being friends. You just wouldn't sleep together any more.

That was my mistake. By the time I realized that there's a difference between friends who have sex and those in romantic relationships, I had broken hearts and been treated very badly by a number of confused and hurt individuals.

Amatonormativity is a term used to describe the assumption that 'a central, exclusive, amorous relationship is normal for humans, in that it is a universally shared goal, and that such a relationship is normative, in that it should be aimed at in preference to other relationship types.'[1] It is the reason no one explains what romance actually means, and why people raise an eyebrow at unmarried adults. Simply put, if you aren't in a relationship, or actively seeking one, you are missing out on something fundamentally human.

My fingers hovered over my phone screen, twitching nervously. I had felt so sure that I was doing the right thing until now. My friends said he deserved to know. He did deserve to know. And, more importantly, I deserved to share something about myself I had only just found the words for.

hey i have something to tell you, i've been doing some research
    and i think i'm aromantic
okay, what does that mean?
i don't experience romantic attraction.

· · · · · · · · · · · · · · · · · ·

1   Granger, R. (2020) 'Amatonormativity, aromanticism, and what defines a relationship.' In *BSU Honors Program Theses and Projects.* Item 330. Accessed on 5/12/2022 at https://vc.bridgew.edu/honors_proj/330

A difficult conversation ensued. What did that mean for us? Well, I didn't want to be with him. Why did things have to change? Couldn't I pretend? Couldn't we work it out? Had I never loved him? Of course I loved him, don't be ridiculous. I loved him as a friend, my best friend. I didn't want that to change. He would need some time, he told me.

> i feel like im making this about me. how are you feeling after finding out?

The phrasing confused me.

> really good, actually. it feels like my entire life makes sense all of a sudden. I didn't realize feeling this way was normal
> oh

I didn't realize until later, but my response disappointed him. He expected me to be heartbroken, I think. That there would be some sense of loss within me, that I would never experience whatever it was I was supposed to. That I would realize that, somehow, I had betrayed him and the trust we had built between us. I didn't feel anything other than joy, if I'm honest. Pure excitement, like the moment in school you stare at a particularly difficult maths equation and, after hours of studying and stress, finally understand it. A brilliant, bright, 'oh!' and you're home. The knowledge that I would never find my soulmate to ride off into the sunset with didn't upset me. I didn't have to do it! I didn't have to get married, or settle down with one person, or date anyone if I didn't want to! I had always considered life as one long series of obligations - it had never occurred to me that I could just make up my own steps as I went along. How could I possibly be heartbroken over that?

Navigating relationships is more difficult when you're on your own, however. I experience sexual attraction, but I'm not sure where it should be placed in the dynamics I cultivate. Attraction should precede a desire to date, surely. But it doesn't. In my case, attraction just precedes desire. My ex-boyfriend was worried I was using him for sex. There wasn't a lot I could do to convince him otherwise, since the marker for authentic expressions of care was, naturally, other forms of physical affection. The kinds I find uncomfortable.

Of course, hugging or holding hands or kissing isn't necessarily reserved for those in monogamous romantic relationships. I have happily spent evenings in a cuddle pile with friends, nestled in duvets and a comfortable late-night haze. The discomfort, the unshakeable wrongness, the romance repulsion, they occur simultaneously with the action as obligation. I have to hold his hand, or I don't really care about him. I have to cuddle him, but I can't do the same with anyone else. It doesn't matter that the actions don't come naturally to me, or I don't get any particular joy out of them. They're proof of something internal. Boxes to check before something is considered right and real. I feel trapped by the concept. There is no difference between how much I care for my friends and how much I care for someone I have sex with – other than the fact I have sex with some of them. My platonic relationships have never been placed lower on a relationship hierarchy; there is no hierarchy. Love isn't something that can just be quantified – I feel it, deeply, for many different people in many different ways.

It's hard to explain aromanticism when I don't have anything else to compare it to. I don't know what it's like to feel romantic attraction, so I don't know how my experiences are different from my peers'.

'How do you know you're not in love with me?' he asked. I'm just not. I never was. I thought I was, in the same way I thought I had to reciprocate when he leaned over, breath heavy with vodka and the sickly sweet scent of cola, and said, 'I think I'm falling in love with you.'

Maybe butterflies just make everyone feel nauseous, I thought. Maybe it feels like dread for everyone.

Becoming single again felt like my entire life fell back into place. I could breathe for the first time in months, years. Alone in my bedroom, I allowed myself to sit back and realize that I had been really very unhappy. In my desperate attempts to find what was missing inside me, I had let the world convince me there was something to be found. The expectation that this discovery would have been heartbreaking to me was so absurd, I hadn't even considered it. Not only was there nothing wrong with the way I felt, but it was celebrated in a community of people. I was allowed to prioritize myself, expected to.

This is one of the biggest lessons to learn from the aromantic community. In all the media we consume, we are taught to wait until we become part of a whole. There is someone out there who will complete us and enrich our lives more than we could possibly imagine. You won't need anyone else, because they're the One. Finding other aromantic people reminded me that the most important person in my life will always be me. And it should always be me. What I want matters in the grand scheme of things, forever and always. The conversations about relationships are enriched by our nuance, our discussions of identity and individuality. We advocate for personal autonomy, and finding something – or someone – that will fulfil you without sacrifice. I had spent years without a way to describe what I was feeling, so had assumed that the discomfort was just a part of a compromise that would ensure a happy life.

I don't feel like that any more. I have never considered myself 'alone' while single, let alone lonely. My friends and I meet for coffee every week, multiple times. We sit close, our thighs pressed together, as we crowd on to the same sofa in a small bar. How many bottles of wine should I bring to Thanksgiving dinner? There will be almost 20 of us. We're going to each need to bring some extra chairs, unless we're happy to crowd on to the living-room floor. There are so many small moments that make my life feel fuller than it ever did while I was forcing myself into relationships. I start knitting a coffee cosy for a friend and can't believe anyone could ever think that someone could be more important to me than this.

Maybe it'll be a while before I can find someone I can have a platonic sexual relationship with. Maybe it won't. Regardless, I feel content. And all of us should feel content, just as we are, by ourselves. Alloromantic people can feel enriched by their romantic relationships, but it should be just that: an enrichment. Relationships should benefit those in them, and I will be eternally grateful for the aromantic community for giving me the voice to teach that to myself.

CHAPTER 2

Could I Be Aro?

Spectrum (*noun*):
A scale between two extreme points
A wide range

In contrast to my emotions regarding Wikipedia's abysmal coverage of aromanticism, I got quite excited about Wikipedia's article on the word 'spectrum'. I wish I could just copy and paste the lot here, but I'm under the impression that's a bit illegal, so I'll summarize with a few snippets:

- A spectrum 'is *not limited* to a specific set of values but can vary across a continuum'.
- The word 'spectrum' was initially used in optics to describe the colours of the rainbow but has since been adapted for other topics like political views, neurodiversity and, of course, orientation. Values within these examples aren't always 'associated with precisely quantifiable numbers or definitions'.[1]

. . . .

1   Wikipedia (2021) 'Spectrum.' Accessed on 3/11/2022 at https://en.wikipedia.org/w/index.php?title=Spectrum&oldid=1052245735

The above basically gives you permission to define your romantic orientation however the hell you want to. Okay, that doesn't necessarily mean that single alloromantic people can claim aromanticism because they're embarrassed to be single (newsflash: being single isn't a bad thing *at all*), but you definitely have permission to explore romantic orientation because, by Wikipedia's definition, it's unlimited.

Labels

Many people find labels to be wholly unnecessary. Some people use them fictitiously to get out of awkward situations – girls claiming to be lesbians just to get guys to stop hitting on them is a prime example. Others just call themselves 'queer' and get on with their lives (respect).

Although I'm not sure if I have a label any more, I personally believe labels can be important for identifying how we feel and finding community. I can't tell you how often I wondered what was wrong with me before finding my labels. The logical part of me knew there *must* be other people like me out there, but the rest of me was determined to train myself to enjoy amatonormative behaviours. (Amatonormativity is a term coined by Professor Elizabeth Brake referring to traditionally romantic relationships and behaviours.[2]) Two memories in particular come to mind. Admittedly, they are more to do with sexual attraction than romantic, but they do go to show that having labels to explain how I felt would've really helped me:

2   Brake, E. 'Amatonormativity.' Accessed on 3/11/2022 at https://elizabethbrake.com/amatonormativity

- I fell in love with a long-distance friend. We acknowledged our feelings for each other but agreed that the distance between us would make everything too hard. However, I still envisioned a relationship with her, except that I wanted a romantic relationship with no sex. I told myself that, of course, she wouldn't agree to that; *everyone* wants sex, don't they? How could we be in a relationship without sex? (Quite easily, Sam of the past, you poor thing.)

- I still feel a level of shame telling this next story, but honestly it's the ex who should be ashamed and not me, so here goes: I was dumped because I was bad at sex. I'm not going to get into it beyond that, even though I have plenty to say about it, because my defences aren't the point here. The point: I was so devastated by this, and so convinced I needed an amatonormative relationship to live my life, that I went on Tinder to find someone to learn sexual competence with. I did a little sum in my head during those dark times: develop trust with new partner + more sex = sexual competence = development of 'normal' sexual attraction levels = being 'normal'. Yikes. I've mentioned I'm bad at maths, right? Needless to say, the lovely fellow I matched with and I didn't last.

Amatonormativity is the idea of a romantic, sexual relationship that eventually leads to marriage, babies, a picket fence and maybe a Labrador. Many of you reading this are probably just imagining grabbing the Labrador and running, right? The thing no one told me back then, however, is that I could pick and choose which of those things belonged in my life, and that there were words for how I felt. Better still, there were people like me in the world and we had a community.

If I'd known this, maybe I never would've felt the need to pick through Tinder for sexual practice. Maybe I'd have given that long-distance sexless relationship a go. It's no use wondering how different my life would've been, but it's nice to think that one day such disasters might be prevented with the widespread knowledge that the A communities exist.

That is why I think labels are important. So, with that said, I want to explore labels a little deeper – because 'aromantic' isn't a label for everyone, even if they're on the aro spectrum. Some aro-spec people feel raging romantic attraction for people until it's reciprocated, and then it goes *poof* – so it could be argued that 'raging romantic attraction' is a bit more than 'little to no romantic attraction', and therefore 'aromantic' doesn't quite fit. Might I suggest 'lithromantic' instead? In contrast, some people only feel romantic attraction once a strong bond has formed with a certain person, and therefore identify as demiromantic. Both of these examples are romantic orientations under the aromantic umbrella.

Micro labels

Using micro labels can be beneficial for people who err on the more complex ends of the aromantic spectrum. The examples I've given above – demiromantic and lithromantic – are commonly used in the aromantic community as easy identifiers for how certain aromantic people feel. The aromantic spectrum is made up of many more of these micro labels, or some people just use aro-spec if none of these quite fit. Below, I've listed a few aromantic micro labels, but there are others, and if you'd like to find your label, I strongly suggest doing a bit of your own research and exploration.

- We'll start with one I will use a lot throughout this book: **alloromantic**. This is basically the opposite of aromantic, meaning you feel romantic attraction. This is what's generally regarded as the norm, along with cisgender and heterosexual, though obviously we're working to change that assumption. I'm assuming the majority of this book's readers do not identify with this label, but it's an important term in the aromantic dictionary.
- **Demiromantic** describes someone who feels romantic attraction only after a bond has been formed. This could mean you make friends with someone, and as your bond strengthens, you start to develop romantic feelings. Alternatively, it could look like a friendship with benefits that you build your romantic attraction on. Many alloromantics are confused by this and claim that it's the same for everyone, but I know for certain that a large percentage of the same people are romantically attracted to Ryan Reynolds and have probably never met him, let alone formed a bond with him. With demiromantic people, usually certain criteria must be met to activate the romantic feelings, whereas alloromantic people can feel them without conditions.
- **Cupioromantic** describes someone who wants to be in a romantic relationship but lacks romantic attraction. We touched on this earlier. It's essentially the same as wanting to have sex but not being attracted to anyone in the room. Would it stop some people from having sex? Absolutely not. I can pinpoint several moments in my life when this label could've come in useful for me.
- **Quoiromantic** refers to someone who cannot wrap their head around the idea of romance. You might be unsure

if you've ever felt romantic attraction because you don't quite understand it, or you might consider the idea of romantic attraction to be utterly ridiculous. You might find it difficult to differentiate between romantic attraction and other types of attraction, and therefore struggle to explain how you're feeling. Some also use this label if they don't know where on the aromantic spectrum they fit. I came across a comment on a subreddit describing this term as 'the agnostics of the aromantic spectrum', which I thought was a clever way of putting it.

- **Lithromantic** describes someone who feels romantic attraction until it's reciprocated (also known as **akioromantic**). You might prefer the butterflies and romantic tension unrequited love provides, but when the object of your affections returns your feelings, you either stop being romantically attracted to them straight away or your attraction may fade over time.

- **Aroflux** can describe someone who fluctuates on the aromantic spectrum. I identified this way for a while, having been unsure if I was feeling romantic attraction towards someone I was close with. Aroflux people can either fluctuate strictly on the aro spectrum or fluctuate between alloromantic and aromantic. In my experience, it was difficult to grasp my identity when I claimed this label, because my feelings would change quite often. Also, this label can come with a lot of misunderstanding on an outsider's part. If, for example, you're feeling closer to demiromantic or alloromantic, people might assume you're no longer aromantic, or, in fact, that you never were, and this can feel invalidating. Just know, it's valid, and there are plenty of people who identify this way and feel comfortable doing so.

- The label **nebularomantic** is very similar to quoiro-mantic; it refers to someone who has trouble distinguishing between romantic and platonic attraction, but it is only used by neurodivergent people. This also comes under another group of orientations referred to as **neurosexuality**, which focuses on orientations affected by neurodivergence. Neurodivergent is defined as describing someone whose brain works a little differently from what is considered 'typical', including but not limited to people with attention deficit hyperactivity disorder (ADHD), autistic people and dyslexic people. Nebularomantic and neurosexual are not terms that should be used by neurotypical people.
- **Fictoromantic** describes romantic attraction towards fictional characters. Presumably, if this character was brought to life through cosplay, or if you saw them acted out in a theatre, your romantic attraction might temporarily wane as they're less fictional when embodied by a real person.
- **WTFromantic**...basically, what it says on the tin. You're really not sure if you fit on the aromantic spectrum or *where* you fit on the aromantic spectrum. I considered taking up this label when my romantic feelings decided to go on a roller coaster in recent months, but it just feels too slang-y for me. I'm aware that that sentence was a bit ironic, and I mean no offence to anyone who chooses to use this label.

These orientations can be paired with any or even multiple sexual orientations. Relationships and emotions are complex things, and having more terminology and understanding of this terminology can be nothing but a good thing.

Liam identifies as pansexual (sexually attracted to people regardless of gender), aromantic and aegoromantic (interested in romance but not interested in partaking in romantic activities):

> When it comes to relationships, I appreciate physical intimacy and close friendships, but I don't experience any romantic feelings. I prefer to date polyamorous people as they can get their romantic needs met in other relationships. I enjoy obsessing over fictional characters in a way that I imagine feels similar to romantic interest (although I can't be entirely sure as I've never experienced romantic feelings), but I know that if the characters magically came to life and expressed interest, those feelings would disappear.

It's also possible for all your other orientations to line up, with the exception of your romantic identity. Maya[3] is a cisgender woman, heterosexual and aromantic. This particular combination of orientations is often portrayed in the media as a negative thing, but a life without romantic feelings isn't necessarily a life completely devoid of love. We'll look more into aromantic portrayals in a later chapter.

> I was born in the late 1970s, and when I hit puberty in the late 1980s, aromanticism was still unknown. Everyone I knew wanted to get married and have children, but I didn't. It was difficult telling my family I didn't want these things. They insisted all it would take was me meeting a nice boy and then I'd be fixed.
>
> Growing up, I didn't know how to flirt or show interest in

3   This name is not the person's real name.

anyone; it felt so alien. Some of my classmates wondered if I was bisexual or a lesbian because I'd never had a boyfriend, but I'd never had a girlfriend, either.

While romance didn't interest me, I was very interested in sex and sexuality. By the age of 18, I had a reasonably large collection of written erotica and pornography. I lusted after men and wanted to begin my sex life – but how could I do that without a boyfriend? Slut-shaming was, and unfortunately still is, very common, and if anyone I knew found out I was feeling this way, I knew that's what they'd think of me. Since then, I've had many sexual encounters, but still never been in a relationship. I've never understood why people feel so strongly about being in love before having sex. Sex is fun and you don't necessarily need romance for it.

Only about three years ago, I discovered aromanticism. It was liberating to know that I'm not a freak of nature – this *is* my nature!

The mini-quiz

Aromanticism is different for every single individual. Some aros are completely romance-repulsed, never feel romantic attraction under any circumstances and will never stray from this. Other aros might feel romantic attraction on very rare occasions, other aros might crave romance but never feel the attraction, and some aros might feel romantic attraction under certain circumstances. This can get a bit confusing – take my case, for example. I broke off a brief courtship because nothing was clicking for me; I didn't want to be sexual or romantic with this person – I just liked the *idea* of it. So when I found the terms 'aromantic' and 'asexual', I thought, 'That's it, that's me.' I identified with those labels for a good few years, and then all sorts of attractions slapped me in the face in recent months, which really threw a spanner in the works. Was this circumstantial or a fluctuation of my orientations? I don't know, but I'm currently still going through it and enjoying it, so I'll go with it.

Orientations, feelings, attraction... It's all complicated. Everyone experiences these things in different ways, so how are you to know who or what you really are? Well, I've made a quiz if that helps. I mean, it's designed for you to look inside yourself, and unfortunately doesn't give definitive answers so it probably doesn't help, but quizzes are fun, right?

Question 1: Who do you have a crush on?

a. A friend

b. My partner

c. A fictional character/celebrity

d. No one

Now, unless you picked 'no one', ask yourself: What sort of crush is this? Is it admiration, idolization, sexual or romantic? How would you like to express these feelings? Do you want to touch this person, hold their hand, kiss them or have sex with them, or are they just pretty?

Question 2: Have you ever wanted to do any
of these things? (Pick all that apply.)

a. Kiss
b. Cuddle
c. Have sex
d. None of the above

It's interesting to wonder if kissing is actually a romantic act. I suppose it depends on your perspective. If you're in a purely sexual relationship, would you kiss the person while you're having sex with them?

Question 3: Consider your answer(s) to the
previous question. Did you have a particular person
in mind who you'd like to do these things with?

a. A friend
b. My partner
c. A fictional character/celebrity
d. No one

Perhaps you want to do the above things, but with no one in particular. Perhaps none of it feels romantic to you; romance might be more of a feeling than an action. If you picked a, b or c for question 2, but d for question 3, this would be a good example of cupioromanticism.

Question 4: Think back to the first question having answered the following two. Do you still think you're crushing on this person? (Skip this question if you answered 'No one'.)

a. Maybe it's more of an intense desire for friendship or admiration
b. Yes, it's a crush
c. Maybe
d. Maybe not

It's okay not to know. It can feel strange when you feel so strongly for someone but can't properly describe those feelings. Until you know for sure, let them know they're important to you. Whatever relationships you maintain as an aro-spec person, it's important to cherish those relationships.

Question 5: Do you crave commitment?

a. Yes
b. No
c. Sometimes
d. Rarely

As mentioned above, any kind of close relationship is an important one. I know I've been guilty of getting jealous when my best friend posts pictures of her and her other friends on social media – like, excuse me, you're *my* friend – but the right people will stay. Commitment doesn't have to be romantic or exclusive.

Question 6: Have you ever fantasized
about being in a romantic relationship or
enjoyed dreams involving romance?

a. Yes

b. Somewhat

c. No

Sit with these thoughts. Are you fantasizing about being in this kind of relationship because so few people understand you and your aromanticism, and because you want to feel 'normal'? A wise villain called Harley Quinn once said, 'Normal is a setting on the dryer.' Don't concern yourself with what other people consider normal; be true to yourself.

If you've enjoyed dreams involving romance, that doesn't necessarily mean that the conscious you wants romance. Sometimes it's nice to slip into an alternate reality and see what you might be like in another life. I've had plenty of dreams about having a baby and absolutely loving it, but I wake up and I'm quite happily without child, thank you very much.

Question 7: What type of relationship
appeals most to you?

a. A romantic relationship

b. Friends with benefits

c. A non-romantic and/or non-sexual soulmate

d. Friendship

Many people in the aromantic community opt for queerplatonic relationships (QPRs), defined very briefly by answer c. We'll look more into this in a later chapter, but if you don't crave romance, it doesn't mean you can't have a partner. If you're one of the people who answered 'yes' to the commitment question, it might be worth looking into QPRs.

Question 8: Do you want to get married?

a. Yes

b. Unsure

c. I want the atmosphere/special day,
but I can take or leave the partner

d. No

I talked about answer c in a YouTube video once. Spending a day looking absolutely stunning in a white dress really appeals to me. If I'm single when that day comes, I'm still going to feel amazing. If I'm in a relationship with someone, yes, I'd also like the ring and the endless, unbreakable commitment.[4]

People get married for many reasons: financial stability, fear of being alone, surprise pregnancies and, of course, undying love. Some are positive reasons, some are negative, some are romantic and some are not. It's completely possible to be aromantic and married.

. . . .

4   This quiz is unexpectedly making me realize that I'm quite possessive...
[*Insert sheepish emoji*].

Question 9: How do you feel about being single?

a. I prefer it
b. I don't mind
c. Unsure
d. I prefer having a significant other

It's worth noting that however you identify romantically, being single is perfectly fine. You can find happiness with or without a significant other. Again, you can crave romance but not feel romantic attraction, so if you answered d, it might be worth asking yourself who you see as your significant other. Then see which answer lines up best with each of the romantic orientations I've outlined above.

Sorry I didn't end the quiz with results. It's designed to make you think for yourself, not tell you who you are. A couple of pages in a book about romantic orientation cannot do that. I mean, if you insist on results...

If you answered mostly a:
You could be on the aromantic spectrum.

If you answered mostly b:
You could be on the aromantic spectrum.

If you answered mostly c:
You could be on the aromantic spectrum.

If you answered mostly d:
You could be on the aromantic spectrum.

Better?

Seriously, though, I encourage you to take a big chunk of time with this quiz. Come back to it, circle things, scribble in the margins, figure yourself out. Come back to it *multiple* times, in fact, because for some people, orientation fluctuates (*cough*) and it could turn out you answer completely differently the next time you take the quiz. Remember to refer to the micro label section, too. See how your answers relate to each label. It doesn't mean you have to commit to these labels; it's just interesting for you to think about.

CHAPTER 3

Aromantic Relationships

I'm glad I never went to the cinema to see Disney's *Ralph Breaks the Internet*. Instead, I watched it on my dad's TV when it came out on DVD. If you're unfamiliar, it's the sequel to *Wreck-It Ralph*, an animated film about arcade game characters living their everyday lives during the arcade's closing hours, and it's relevant, I promise. In *Ralph Breaks the Internet*, Vanellope, one of the two main characters, finds excitement in a new game which her best friend Ralph won't always have access to. Ralph takes this separation hard, while Vanellope is enthusiastic about this new venture. At the end (spoiler alert), the two friends go their separate ways, they hug goodbye, and Vanellope tearfully says, 'I love you so much.' And that was it, I was bawling *hard* in front of my entire family. It was the kind of crying I'd have been ashamed to do in the cinema.

I watched that film while my aromanticism was going strong, and for that reason I was extremely attached to my close friends. My biggest fear was being left behind by those people, because all of them are alloromantic and either in relationships or seeking them. That scene really brought my fear to life, and although it's Disney's way of saying you need to prioritize yourself and your own dreams, and that true friends will stay in touch unconditionally, what I took from it was that those two best friends were splitting up, and that wasn't how I wanted life to work. Unfortunately, a lot of the time, that's exactly how life works, but, like I said, the best people will never leave you completely.

It's a common fear among aromantic people that they'll end up alone while all their loved ones swan off in romantic relationships, start families and forget all about them. The important thing to realize here is that *all relationships are important*. There's this unspoken but common belief that romantic relationships are the Ultimate Relationship, that they're somehow more important than friendships, family relationships and any other kind of relationship. But ask yourself this: If that Ultimate Relationship crumbles, what's left? That's right: your friends and family. So why do people prioritize a relationship that isn't always guaranteed to be permanent?

Admittedly, I've been guilty of prioritizing relationships with a significant other over my other relationships on more than one occasion. It's easy to get swept up in it. But when you prioritize one relationship, others suffer. You might lose touch with a friend or get into arguments with your family because you're not seeing them as much. Maybe your work colleagues will get sick of you constantly ducking out of conversations to text your partner or missing out on outings because you'd rather go out with your partner, and as a result the important connections with your colleagues suffer. It's something that's hard to juggle, but the thing aromantic people understand better than anyone is that it's so vital to cherish all your connections.

Family connections are ones you assume are unbreakable, but as you grow up, you realize that's not the case. There's no rule that says you have to keep the peace with your family members if you clash, or even that you have to love your family. Families are all different. But if you're fortunate, like me, and your family is close and supportive, appreciate those relationships. These are the first relationships you'd have ever formed. These relationships might have taught you how to communicate, how to form bonds and how to love. Don't just assume they'll always be there and don't take them for granted. As an aro-spec person, you might not find or seek a significant other, but your nan will always be there for a cup of tea and a gossip. Put this book down right now and go drop her a bunch of flowers – but come back quick, because we've got a lot more to cover!

Friendships come and go – that's an absolute given. I've not retained any friendships from primary school, and I've kept one friend from secondary school. Admittedly, there are some hierarchies when it comes to friendship; you'll have your friends you go out with on occasion to have a laugh with, but you don't tell them your deepest, darkest secrets, and you'll have your best friends who you'll ugly-cry with. The longevity of a friendship is never guaranteed, but while you're friends with someone, make sure you appreciate that relationship. I have a best friend whom I've known for 16 years, and I see her once or twice a year, but we write to each other, and we know that we'll never fall out. She'll always be one of the most important people in my life. I have a friend who I haven't been close with for very long, but we're so affectionate with each other, and I moan his ear off and he never complains. He likes stealing my work hat and keeping it hostage overnight, and we are very enthusiastic about dogs, and I cherish him as much as I cherish my friend of 16 years. Time doesn't always equal importance, just like romance shouldn't mean superiority.

Work colleagues are also surprisingly important as you go through life. Friendships often develop from work environments, but even if your friendships don't extend beyond the workplace, they're still important. You could potentially be spending most of your time in the workplace, so it's nice to get along with your colleagues. There are so many different types of work relationships, too – like the work mother who will make you take a break if you need one and will ensure you eat something, or the work brothers who you can have an absolute hoot with, or a colleague that you just chill with and give little shoulder rubs to when they look stressed. Honestly, if you love the people you work with, your life is automatically better. The great thing about socializing in work as an aro-spec person is that all romance is removed. Yes, people who work together may be in romantic relationships, but the professional environment can and should remove that aspect while you're all clocked in. So you're all on equal ground, enjoying each other's company, and there's some respite from all that amatonormative crap you might be trying to avoid as an aromantic person. It's just a bonus if you're friends outside of work, too!

Online connections are nice to have in this day and age. Personally, I don't put *as much* stock in them as I do face-to-face relationships, but some people do, and that can be a good thing. I personally prefer being in the presence of my peeps, because typing all the time can be exhausting (she says while she types an entire book), and certain things can be misconstrued – especially if you forget to drop an emoji to illustrate your tone. I keep in contact with a few people online – childhood friends, friends with chronic illnesses who maybe can't make it out to see me face to face, distant family members – and I know those people are always there if I need them, which is nice. A lot of people in my generation and the generations after mine do have online friends whom they've never met, and it's pretty cool that you can have a best friend who lives in Hawaii. You might tell this person everything, and they might be there for you in a way that your nan can't be, and that's important. You always need someone to confide in, and if that person is a physical stranger, that's fine. Just make sure you're careful and you don't send them money or nude photographs. That might've come across as a joke, but I mean it. Be safe online.

Friends with benefits can be fun, and they're an option for any allosexual[1] aromantic person who's not looking for a partner. This can be primarily sexual, or the person can be your best friend who you occasionally let off some steam with. This is the sort of relationship that requires a lot of communication; you need to establish boundaries, check in with each other, be honest and stay sure of where you stand. It can be easy to get hurt or hurt the other person if your communication isn't clear. It could be a temporary bit of fun, or it could even last forever if neither of you is particularly interested in a romantic partner. Amatonormativity in society can mean you and this friend might be judged, or people might just *insist* that you're in a relationship, but at the end of the day, you're having fun, you're not hurting anyone, and it's no one's damn business.

The lowdown: every relationship is important. Think of

. . . .

1   Reminder: allo means you feel attraction. So allosexual means you feel sexual attraction. Also, it's important to note you don't have to be allosexual to enjoy a sexual relationship.

each relationship as a plant. You wouldn't just water *one* and let the others die, would you? Speaking of *one*, there's one type of relationship I haven't mentioned here...

Queerplatonic relationships

This type of relationship needs its own subsection because it's a very aro-specific relationship that not everyone will understand with a simple paragraph. I mentioned it briefly on a previous page, but the basic definition of a QPR is a significant other or life partner with whom you may not be romantically or sexually involved. Maybe you could call it 'platonic marriage' for argument's sake – although obviously you don't have to marry the person you're in this kind of partnership with if you don't fancy it. Maybe the people of Twitter can explain it better:

> As far as I understand, a QPR is a non-romantic committed relationship. The specifics depend on people in the relationship.

The above is a good definition: to the point, and better than mine. And I call myself a writer (sigh). You can be in a queerplatonic relationship, but it could be open, and your QPP (that's queerplatonic partner) might have sexual or romantic relationships outside of your partnership. Alternatively, you might commit exclusively to this person. It's all up to you and your person.

> It's a partnership that transcends a traditional friendship... Basically a relationship without the romantic expectations.

Not abiding to societal norms of what a platonic relationship entails, where the parties involved set the expectations and commitments based on mutual benefits and well-being.

A QPR is one of many answers to an aromantic person's fear of ending up alone. It might not be for everyone, and I'm guessing they're difficult to find, because two people won't just automatically fall in platonic love *purely* because they're aromantic. It is, however, in my personal opinion, such a cool thing. I get that having a 'person' might seem possessive and old-fashioned to some people, but many of us *need* that commitment; some of us need the reassurance that we're wanted and loved, even if not in the traditional way.

Single as heck

I suppose it's also important to mention your relationship with yourself here. It's commonly said that the only guaranteed constant in your life is you, which I firmly believe. You can be deeply in love with whatever kind of partner you have, but as drastic and awful as it sounds, they might not be alive tomorrow. So you have to cherish your people while you can but remember the guaranteed constant: you.

Take care of yourself. Take yourself on a harbourside walk. Treat yourself to ice cream. There are many moments I've cherished in my life that I've experienced all by myself, however small, such as the hours spent painting portraits with a vinyl record spinning behind me, or watching every episode of *She-Ra and the Princesses of Power* by myself and crying when it ended.

The relationship you have with yourself is one people tend

to forget about, but it's so important. If you're an aromantic person with no interest in any sort of partnership, or if you're even just a single alloromantic person, it's easier to prioritize your relationship with yourself. As I've said before, being single isn't a bad thing, and it can really help you grow a healthy relationship with yourself as well as providing other benefits to you:

- **Operating on your own timescale.** You don't need to consider another person's schedule when deciding what time you're going to eat dinner or when you're setting your alarm for the next morning.
- **A bed to yourself.** Those of us in relationships would always insist they'd rather sleep with their partners, but having the entire bed to yourself at night can provide you with the ultimate comfort and a great night's sleep.
- **It's cheaper.** Dates are expensive, and although being in a relationship can cheapen over time as you grow comfortable in each other's spaces, date night always tends to be a thing in a traditional romantic relationship.
- **Less anxiety.** Jealousy rears its ugly head in all relationships at some point. Plus, you're constantly worrying about your appearance. When you're single, you can wear tracksuit bottoms for a week, and no one will say anything!
- **You're a better friend.** No matter how hard you try to spend as much time with your friends as before, it's unlikely to happen when you're in a relationship; you're often dividing your time between them, which can unfortunately mean friendships take a hit.

To those who believe romance-repulsed aromantics are sad

and lonely, please read the above and know you're wrong. Aro-spec people who opt out of committed relationships are often very happy in themselves and their lives, plenty self-sufficient and perfectly independent. If you're in a relationship yourself, that's great, and it has plenty of benefits, too, but it doesn't mean to say people who choose to be single are miserable.

The aro experience

Every single relationship is different. The term 'significant other' probably has an infinite number of meanings, because it means something different to everyone. Even if you're cisgender (the gender you were assigned at birth) and straight, your relationship will not look exactly the same as your cisgender straight friends' relationships. Relationships involving one or multiple aromantic people are even more diverse.

Rachel,[2] for example, is looking for a specific kind of significant other:

> I used to identify as 'greyaro', but now I prefer 'aro-spec' because I'm exploring the possibility that I might be demiromantic. I have no intention of coming out in real life to anyone except my partner, but I haven't been with anyone since realizing I was aro-spec and I'm not sure how to do it.
>
> To me, a partnership would look like a more-than-friends[3]

---

2 This name is not the person's real name.
3 Just a reminder that this book supports the idea of all relationships being equal, so if the term 'more than friends' crops up, think of the word 'more' as a quantity, not quality.

relationship without the romance. For me that means no formal dates or special dinners, no getting married, and living separately. To me, flirting and kissing are sexual, so as a heterosexual I'm comfortable doing those things with a sexual partner.

I think things like sleeping in the same bed or raising a child are things that are neither sexual nor romantic, but when the topic of children comes up in aro spaces, everyone says they see it as tied to marriage and romance. Under the right circumstances, I'd happily have a child and raise it on my own.

I also identify as arogender (a gender that you feel is intrinsically connected to your aromanticism), and this label is important to me because not only is there a stereotypically 'women's' culture around romance that I'm not a part of, I also dislike oppositional sexism (the belief that 'male' and 'female' is a rigid binary). In hetero romance, the man is expected to be the provider/protector who actively initiates the relationship, and the woman is the one he's supposed to do all that for. When my significant other is hugging me, I don't think about how delicate and safe I feel, but how good the activity feels and how happy I am.

I'm sharing my story because I know that most aromantics are also asexual, and I want to spread awareness that that is not always the case.

Liz[4] sought out something similar, and through trial and error in her previous relationships, she is now happy with her queerplatonic partner:

I grew up in a conservative, religious household. I didn't have

----

4   This name is not the person's real name.

crushes on boys, so in middle school I asked my best friend to pick boys for me to like, because I couldn't decide.

I started dating a guy when I was 17. This relationship helped me realize I'm not completely asexual, and I now identify as demisexual, though I didn't have a word for it at the time. We broke up when I moved away, but I still keep in contact with him. I've come to realize that as an aro-spec person it's quite easy to stay friends with exes.

I met my QPP when I was 18 years old. We went from friends to lovers to roommates and we got married for financial reasons. I didn't enjoy the wedding itself. I didn't want to change my name, I didn't want the dress, the awkward dancing or anything else that comes with a traditional wedding. We were non-monogamous, and one partner I had actually convinced me to leave him because I couldn't possibly love him if I was having sex with other people, could I?

Fortunately, after two more failed marriages, my QPP came back into my life. We consider ourselves family, the best of friends and roommates. Some have tried to imply that we are a couple, but we are not romantically or sexually involved. I don't know what else to say other than he is my person. He's free to come and go as he pleases and so am I.

Mattea is another aro-spec person who felt trapped and confused in an amatonormative relationship. They, like many aros, were led to believe that they should be in a romantic relationship, even if it didn't feel right. They mention below that they'd been waiting for a 'reason' to break up with their ex-partner because being unhappy didn't feel reason enough. Please, if you're in a relationship and it doesn't feel right, *communicate*. There is no rule that says you have to stay in a relationship if it doesn't feel right. You don't need a 'solid reason'. Any reason you have is legitimate, but communication is *always* key.

> I was 16 when my friend G asked me out. At first, I thought they were joking and I laughed, but when I realized they were serious, I said yes because I wanted to see what dating was like. At the beginning I didn't realize being in a relationship made me unhappy and uncomfortable, but as the two years progressed, I slowly started to connect the dots.
>
> I went to numerous dances with G, but when prom rolled around, they were out of town so I went with my friends, and I noticed the differences straight away. I enjoyed dancing with my friends, I didn't feel awkward, and it was the most fun I'd had at a dance since I started dating G. I started dreading every date that we would plan, and I would make sure the dates were always at G's house so I could leave whenever I wanted.
>
> When G told me they loved me, I said it back because *that's what you're supposed to do when someone tells you they love you.* I eventually realized that it wasn't actually true, so I stopped saying it back.
>
> While we were dating, I wrote a sort of journal entry in my phone that I never planned to share with anyone. I wrote about feeling broken because of my asexuality and what I wanted in a relationship. I must have known about aromanticism at that point because there's a line that says, 'Sometimes I think that makes me aromantic, but I still want a relationship.'
>
> Eventually, I broke up with G. They'd been expecting it. Part of the reason it took me such a long time to finally break up with them is because I felt like I needed a 'real' reason to break up with them. *I didn't think that being unhappy was a good enough reason to end a relationship.*

It was that summer that I came to terms with my aromanticism. Admittedly, years later, I'm still trying to fully accept it, and I still don't know exactly where on the aromantic spectrum I fall.

That same summer, I was spending a lot of time with one of my friends, Z. She was the first person I came out as aromantic to. We'd been friends for a long time, and we were about to go to college together. Throughout that school year, we spent a lot of time together: between classes, on weekends, and during the spring semester we were in a musical together. We still saw our other friends at various points throughout the year and during the summer, but we tended to gravitate toward each other more than we had previously.

There was one weekend the summer after our freshman year of college we were at a local farmer's market with our friends. We were talking to two of our friends and made some joke about us being queerplatonic partners. It wasn't the first time we talked about QPRs or even whether or not we were in one. We didn't really talk about it much again that day, but I remember thinking about it a lot. Maybe a few weeks later, we decided to actually put a label to our QPR. Everything felt, and feels, so different in this relationship. First is the fact that this isn't a romantic relationship. The other is part of the reason I'm questioning where exactly I fall on the aromantic spectrum: in the past year or so, I've started questioning how I experience other types of attraction. For a long time, I identified as pansexual, and then panromantic (attracted to someone regardless of gender). And then when I figured out that I fall on the aromantic spectrum, I just kind of assumed that was it. But then talking to other a-spec people, I started thinking about aesthetic and queerplatonic attraction. I settled on lesbian-oriented, which I guess confuses people since I'm also under the non-binary umbrella. I don't really have a good explanation for what the lesbian label means to me other than it just fits better than other labels.

I haven't thought about it fully, but I've had fleeting moments of 'What if I'm not actually aromantic, but I really just haven't met the right person?' I'm definitely not romantically attracted to Z, but sometimes I think about dating other people in an abstract way. *It's hard to know if that's something I actually want or if it's because romantic relationships are so ingrained in society.*

Z is my best friend. We go on platonic dates and they make me so much happier than dates with G ever did. We've officially been in our QPR for a little over two years, longer than I was with G. It's weird being in a QPR because most people don't know what they are. I usually hesitate to call her my partner when people don't know I'm aromantic, because then they would assume we're dating and the thought of that makes me uncomfortable. We do a lot of things that people would probably consider romantic – we cuddle and hold hands, go on dates – but for us it's not romantic, it's just how we are with each other.

I'm going to reiterate: a significant other is no more important than a friend. All relationships are important. Aromantic or not, it's good to be happy being single. Having a partner of any description can be amazing, sure, but being happy with yourself should come first. After several attempts at an amatonormative relationship, Amy[5] discovered this for herself:

I started properly dating in college, and every single relationship went the same way. It would start off fine; we'd go on

---

5   This name is not the person's real name.

fun dates, maybe share a kiss or two... But as soon as it got serious, I would completely freak out. I would turn my phone on flight mode just to avoid their texts. I would make flimsy excuses to avoid dates. The thought of holding their hand was nauseating. The thought of them touching me was horrifying.

And it wasn't their fault; they hadn't done anything wrong. All they had done was told me they liked me, but it was like a switch flicking in my brain. I just suddenly felt extremely claustrophobic by the entire situation, and I had to get out of it.

Then I met someone who didn't want a relationship. We decided to try a friends-with-benefits relationship, and it worked. They never told me they liked me, never tried to ask me out on a date. We just had fun. We were best mates with all the extras. It was great; I learned so much about myself, my self-confidence sky-rocketed, I had a stress release, I had someone I could talk to about intimate stuff without the pressure of the other stuff, without romantic expectations. The arrangement didn't last, but we're still friends, and it was amazing while it lasted.

As time passed, I had a few more failed relationships and eventually stumbled across the word 'lithromantic': someone who is repulsed by reciprocated attraction. It was like a lightbulb flicking on. Suddenly, everything made sense: that disgust at being liked, that confusing change in feelings a few months into dating, that comfort with something as intimate as a friends-with-benefits relationship but not able to hold their hand going for coffee...

That was me. That was all me. And I wasn't broken, I wasn't weird, and there were a hundred people just like me who felt the same way. Those failures weren't my fault. I shed almost a decade's worth of guilt in an afternoon. Just because of a word.

I haven't really mentioned it to people. I don't feel the

need. I haven't changed. I'm still the same person I was ten years ago, just now with a name to explain why I do the things I do, why I feel the way I do. It has helped me much better manage and understand my feelings, though. I know now to be careful if I ever get into a relationship again. I know the triggers and warning signs to look out for so I don't hurt my partner. I know better what I want from a relationship and now I'm able to communicate that to any potential partners.

I don't have a partner now. I don't plan on getting one any time soon. But I'm not worried about it.

Where can I find a QPP?

It's completely valid if you're fulfilled and happy in your familial and platonic relationships but still want your own special person. I suppose it's like having the most substantial, tasty and filling meal ever, but you still want dessert. I know when I felt at my most aromantic, I wondered how the hell I would go about finding a queerplatonic partner if I ever wanted to. Barely anyone knows what they are, so how can anyone hope to find one?

The stories in this chapter might give you hope that you'll find one organically, but not everyone is that lucky. Social media has made *real* social interaction difficult. It's easy to give someone a difficult or nerve-wracking piece of information over text because you don't have to see their reaction. It's easier to type than to speak, so communication is harder now more than ever.

So if you're too anxious to physically put yourself out there, there are actually a few places online where you might find a connection with someone.

Facebook is surprisingly good at connecting people. I

know a lot of people think Facebook is a space for middle-aged mothers to slate their neighbours and the local youths, and for grandparents to post pictures of their cruises and tag absolutely everyone they know for no reason at all, but there are limitless communities on there once you've unsubscribed from Grandma. It's really simple, too: I literally just typed 'aromantic' into the Facebook search bar, clicked on groups and found results. One group I joined a while back when I was curious about QPRs is called 'Queer Platonic Aromantic Connections (QPAC)'.[6] This is a group where people post a short bio, a picture and what they're looking for in a QPR, and see where things go from there. I have never posted or responded to anyone on there, so I don't know about success rates, but it seems like a good place to start. The groups on Facebook don't have a massive number of members each, but you never know whom you might meet.

Reddit is also a good place to look. Again, I just typed 'QPR' into the search bar and found a page called 'r/qprapplications', which does exactly what it says on the tin.[7] You post your labels, your age, where you're from and what you're looking for in a QPR, then await responses or respond to existing posts. There are also communities on Reddit for all things aromantic, not just finding a partner. Bear in mind it took me five seconds each to find the Facebook page and the Reddit page. That's a lot of possibility in a very short space of time, so there's hope. Imagine what you could do with an hour!

Apparently, there are also a lot of dating apps that allow you to simply search for friendships, but I've never been on them

6   Queer Platonic Aromantic Connections (QPAC) group on Facebook. Accessed on 7/11/2022 at www.facebook.com/groups/6259957908180016

7   QPR applications on Reddit. Accessed on 7/11/2022 at www.reddit.com/r/qprapplications

so I cannot confirm. However, there is a website specifically for asexual people looking for a partner, and I *can* confirm that many people on this site are seeking a QPP. **Asexuals.net**[8] is a site I signed up to when I was feeling particularly lonely and confused, and there are a lot of lovely people on there. Yes, it's specifically for asexual people, but there are plenty of aromantic people, too, and it's definitely worth signing up.

But if you *are* one of the rare few who prefers meeting people in real life, maybe try going to **LGBT+ events near you.** I was part of a local LGBT+ Facebook group back when I lived in Bristol, and we'd all go to pub quizzes or on walks, and it was a great way to get to know people who lived near me.

Another option, and an obvious one: **Pride.** Yes, it only rolls around once a year, but I lost count of the number of a-spec flags I saw when I went to my last Pride festival. Pride gives you a free pass to talk to absolutely anyone, because we're all there to be happy and celebrate community. Obviously, if they're looking standoffish, maybe don't engage, but you know what I mean. I didn't approach anyone when I went to Pride because I was with my own people, but I *promise* that if you go and you see a cluster of people waving aromantic flags, you can approach them and they'll accept you without hesitation.[9] Alternatively, buy an aromantic flag, walk around with it, and I bet someone will talk to you or at least *wave* at you because you're one of them. I was approached and asked what my flag meant at my first Pride, and although it sparked neither a lengthy conversation nor a friendship of any kind, it's proof that conversations and connections can happen just because you're holding a flag. Not only is Pride one of the best days of

. . . .

8   Asexuals dating site. Accessed on 7/11/2022 at www.asexuals.net
9   You have permission to TP my house if my promise falls through.

the year, but it's also a day when it's practically the law to be nice to one another – like Christmas, but in summer!

Who knows? If you're truly blessed you might just **meet your QPP by accident**, but if you don't want to wait for that day, it's time to be proactive. Get out there!

My relationships

I know I've established many times now (and it's only Chapter 3!) that I've kind of shed all my labels, but I just want to further my point here that no two relationships are the same, especially if you're part of the A communities. Maybe I've always fallen somewhere on the aromantic spectrum, and maybe my place on it fluctuates over time – I don't know. But I do know that, up until recently, my relationships have never been amatonormative, and different people have had different things to offer. I think the aim of this part is just to give you a more detailed idea of how vastly relationships differ from each other.

I've always been generally romance-positive. For me, this means I'm open to a relationship for myself if one ever presents itself, or if I'm feeling particularly aromantic, I'm romance-positive for other people – I'll cheerlead my loved ones in their own quests to find love. In spite of this, I honestly don't remember ever fancying anyone right off the bat. You know in films when one character sees another for the first time and there's a pink tinge on the screen, birds are singing and harps are playing because *just like that* they've got a new crush? Yeah, that's never happened to me. Looking back, I think attraction of the sexual or romantic kind has always come to me slowly, if at all, and I'm damn lucky if I feel all

71

the attractions towards one singular person (and to be honest, they're lucky, too, because I can't lie, I *am* wife material).[10]

When I was 15, I got into a relationship with a boy. I'm using the word 'relationship' very loosely here: it was very brief and literally just consisted of hand-holding and texting. One day I wanted to take things to the next level because that's what you're supposed to do (where have we read *that* before?), so when we were due to part ways after walking home from school, I just stood there staring at him like a complete weirdo. My brain was going, 'Kiss him, kiss him', but the rest of me was like, '*Hell* no!' So after standing awkwardly for a minute or so, I ran off and texted him that I was sorry for being weird. Needless to say, that relationship didn't last; he came out as gay after leaving school, and I...well...heh!

My first real relationship was with a girl, Elle (no, that's not her real name). I was 16, I'd come to the realization that none of the boys at school did it for me, so I figured maybe I was into girls. And who better to get into a relationship with than my girl best friend who was openly a lesbian? I wasn't sure if I even liked her when we got together. If I remember correctly, I wrote, 'I think I like you' very small on the corner of a piece of paper – looking back, I know 'think' was the operative word. We entered into a relationship that was argumentative and sexually one-sided. I think, looking back, I was never romantically or sexually attracted to her, but my hormones dictated that I liked being touched, and she claimed not to mind that I didn't want to reciprocate. I don't know

....

10 That's not to say you're *unlucky* if you don't feel all the attractions. If you're romance-repulsed, I'm sure you wouldn't be feeling lucky if romantic attraction all of a sudden presented itself to you. I'm speaking on a personal level here.

how to label my relationship with Elle; I mean, it was both sexual and romantic at times, so I guess it was, by definition, a sexual/romantic relationship, but I don't think the attraction was really there. I was just confused at that point. I guess this is a good example of how aromantic people can be in romantic relationships without feeling that attraction – just maybe remove all the anxiety and add a bit more communication and you're cooking with gas!

I think I was 19 when I entered into my next relationship. I worked in a post office at that point, and most of our customers lived locally so they were regulars. Will (also not his name) was one of those regulars, and *I really liked the way he dressed*. He looked as if he was in a punk rock band – you know the type. I added him on Facebook and asked him out on a date, and we went to a park a few days later. We were both *awkward* and shy, but he kissed me at the end of our date, and from then on, in spite of a very mediocre kiss and a severe lack of sparks, we were together. Because of the awkwardness and shyness, however, most of our conversations took place online, so naturally I was completely terrified to tell him I'd never had sex with a boy before. I didn't particularly want to have sex with Will, but *that's what you did*, right? So I wrote him a letter explaining, and he dumped me over Messenger. I don't remember being particularly upset; in fact, I was relieved. If you're wondering why '*I really liked the way he dressed*' is in italics, that's because the only attraction I felt for Will was aesthetic – I liked the way he looked. Obviously, I didn't know that back then; I thought because I liked the way he looked, I must fancy him, but that was not the case. Things were awkward between us because I did not, in fact, fancy him.

In the time between getting dumped by Will and my next relationship, there were two people of note. The first was another regular post office customer, Chester.[11] Somehow Chester got my number and we started texting, and eventually he asked me out to the cinema. At the time, I had no friends, and my mum and sister were at work all the time, and I was feeling desperately lonely, so I said yes, but the day came and I spent every single minute *sobbing*. Lovely as he was, I didn't want to go out with Chester. I put it down to him being extremely tall and having a kid, but I know that wasn't it. I just wasn't attracted to him.

The second person, Noah,[12] was the first person I ever felt real romantic attraction for. She was a long-distance best friend who I met up with whenever we could afford it. We'd spend several nights together, and we were very close – physically and emotionally. I started to realize I had romantic feelings for her, and I knew as these feelings came to light that sexual feelings didn't come with them. I really liked Noah, but I never knew back then that a romantic relationship without sex was possible, so in spite of her reciprocating my romantic feelings, we decided to stay friends.

I was 21 when I met Graham.[13] At this point in my life, I was so lonely that I turned to Gumtree of all places to find friends. I was that desperate; I didn't even know Gumtree was ever used to find connections, but it was literally my last hope, and, lo and behold, there was one single advertisement on the site seeking friendship. I met Graham in person after exchanging emails for a short time, and eventually we got together. I don't remember feeling romantically or sexually attracted to Graham, but I figured that might come once we'd

. . . .

11 This name is not the person's real name.
12 This name is not the person's real name.
13 This name is not the person's real name.

tackled the sex hurdle. I was transparent with Graham about my sexual inexperience, and he was sweet about it. Once we'd sealed the deal, however, the sparks still failed to come. We split up not long after that.

My final relationship before I discovered aromanticism and asexuality was born on Tinder. We matched, we went on our first date, and he kissed me. It's not the sort of speed I've ever been comfortable with, but *that's what normal people did*, right? I didn't feel attracted to this person, but we kissed on our first date and entered into a relationship straight away. I think over time I developed *some* romantic feelings for my Tinder boyfriend, but I only ever kept our sexual relationship alive because I knew he wanted to. I told myself, not for the first time, that all the feelings 'normal' people felt would come eventually. They did not, and thus, without going into too much detail, the most painful breakup I've ever experienced ensued. I may not have felt every type of attraction for him, but I did love him, and that's the important thing: *aromantic and asexual people are fully capable of love*, and heartbreak and loss aren't synonymous with romantic love.

After that, I scoured Tinder for my next 'romantic' venture. Only, I was starting to become very aware that I wasn't feeling any of the things I was supposed to be feeling for any of these people. You know the next part already, so I'll keep it brief: that was when I had that conversation with my sister in the bathroom about being asexual. That was when I discovered asexuality and aromanticism, and that was when I claimed those labels for myself.

I spent three years finding my place under the asexual and aromantic umbrellas, perfectly content to never enter into a relationship again. I made countless loud-and-proud videos about my labels, I wrote an article for the *Metro* about my complete lack of sexual and romantic attraction, and I went to Pride equipped with the appropriate flags. Yes, I was a bit scared of ending up alone, but I was happy. I had my community, and I had people to relate to.

And then, in late 2021, I changed. I moved out of my home town to a completely new place., I met new people, and I got into new romantic relationships. The first was brief, and I'm not entirely proud of how it ended, but the second is the one that completely ripped the carpet from under me. It began as a friendship, and although I'd have been blind not to notice how handsome he was, a friendship was all it was because I'd just left a relationship that didn't feel right. I was still convinced I was aromantic and asexual, and that my last relationship had ended because of those orientations. So when this friend and I started flirting, it was very confusing for me. I really had to sit down and ask myself what I was feeling for this person, and eventually I settled on sexual attraction, so we became friends with benefits. It only took me two months to realize I was also romantically attracted to him.

As I'm writing this part, he and I are in a relationship and I'm completely in love with him. I'm still a bit perplexed as to how or why it happened, or what I am, or if I even belong in the LGBT+ community any more. But I've lost count of the number of times in my life when I've had to come out, so yesterday, on 8th May 2022, I announced on Twitter that I'd dropped all my labels. Part of me still feels as though I'm betraying the communities I was such an active spokesperson for not too long ago, but the other part of me just wants to live. One thing I do know, though, is that for those years I identified as aromantic and asexual, that was how I felt at the time. Who I am now doesn't invalidate who I was back then, and I know that for most of my life, even if I didn't have the words, I was aromantic and asexual.

Can I make it work?

It's not unheard of to be aromantic and want a romantic relationship, and it's entirely possible. QPRs aren't the only relationships defined by the people in them; every relationship works this way. As long as you're being yourself, you establish clear boundaries and you communicate often, any kind of relationship can work for you.

One of the hardest things is making an alloromantic partner understand that even if you're not romantically attracted to them, it doesn't mean you don't love them as much as you're able. It's easy for someone to take it personally if your attractions don't line up with theirs. It's understandable to worry that your prospective partner might develop some self-esteem issues and question why you're not attracted to them in that way, but they just need reminding that it's not them; it's the way you are. Aromantic people love just as deeply as alloromantic people – just not in all the same ways.

On having kids

Having children is a topic often brought up in aromantic conversations. Again, amatonormativity probably has a hand in this: having children is one of the things you'd tick off the amatonormative 'ideal relationship' checklist along with marriage, pets and a family home. Of course, having kids is something stereotypically associated with being in a couple, so it's understandable that an alloromantic outsider would question whether their aromantic friend would want kids, but having children isn't necessarily a romantic thing. Then again, a quick search on the aromantic subreddit found me a poll asking the aros of Reddit if they'd consider having children, and only 8 out of 113 people voted yes, with 48 on the fence.

Aromantic people can have kids for multitudes of reasons: because they want kids, because they didn't realize their labels until after they'd gotten into relationships and had kids, or because they'd entered into unprotected sexual relationships and only realized they wanted kids when it happened accidentally. For a lot of people, having children doesn't always include a partner.

I asked the aro-spec people of Twitter how they feel about having kids, and here are the responses I got:

Big nope for me all around. But it does suck that so much of adulthood assumes everyone wants kids so even if you say you want to stay single, people immediately rush in to say it's okay to be a single parent and you can always adopt! Ma'am, I can barely be trusted with plants.

Skyler

I'm childfree but I don't think it's related to my aromanticism.

Lisa

Having kids seems like an idea I go back and forth on. Will I ever have kids, I do not know; the responsibility is a lot. I think more about fostering or adoption personally.

Ess

As Lisa said, having children isn't inherently related to your orientation, but in society things like starting a family are so entwined with marriage and romantic relationships that it can be confusing for a third party when an aromantic person wants children. Many aromantic people prefer solitude and being child free, but just as many either consider having kids in the future or definitely want them, and that doesn't make them any less aro.

The Need to Feel Wanted

by C.D.

I never really had much of a dating life until college. When I did start dating in college, I fell into what I'd call 'serial monogamy'. I was just so happy to feel wanted that I ignored countless red flags and fell into incredibly toxic relationships. Often, I was so beaten down or scared to break up (or scared of being alone) that I would stay in these relationships until the last possible second, and jump ship to the next person. I felt at the time like I was in love with these partners; instead, it just masked the fear of being alone. Which is why as soon as a 'better' relationship came into my life, I would leave. I'm not proud at all of how I handled this.

However, when I was in my last year of college, I began seeing someone who I was convinced I was going to marry. She was amazing: smart, funny, beautiful, creative, talented, ambitious, driven, open-minded... To this day, I cannot identify a flaw with her. It was during my three years with her that I began to realize something wasn't 'right'.

Despite us having a lot in common – similar interests, person-alities, humour and overall goals – I never really felt happy in the relationship. I enjoyed going on dates and hanging out with her, but

I kept thinking there was something missing, something that didn't feel completely right. She was very in love with me in the full romantic sense. She loved all the romantic gestures. I didn't mind them, but they didn't really do much for me, at least not in the way they did for her.

I had always thought that the reason I wasn't happy or content in previous relationships was because they were abusive, manipulative or (sometimes) outright cruel to me. However, here I was, with a perfect partner, and I kept finding issues. They manifested as jealousy, petty fights, and eventually we drifted apart romantically and split up. We've stayed friends, but I hold so much regret over how our relationship unfolded.

It was at this time (and in my next relationship) that it started to really click for me that something about traditional relationships wasn't for me. What really did it was a simple realization: that I couldn't view my partner as someone more special to me than anyone else. No matter how hard I tried, I couldn't feel that romantic connection. I enjoyed my next relationship, but I couldn't view it in the romantic context that they could. I'm not romance-repulsed, so I can still participate in romantic activities, but they just never did anything for me. Now that I was older, I was more confident, I had come into my own, and I had lots of connections in my life, so that need/ significance I had put on feeling 'wanted' by a partner was faded, and I could more clearly discern that I couldn't really generate romantic feelings, no matter how hard I tried.

Once the veil of 'needing to feel wanted' was gone, I could fully step back and decide what relationships I could have. That 'wanted' feeling was really the only thing that kept me connected to these partners, and the only thing that had really elevated them. Once it faded, I made clear that there were romantic imbalances that I couldn't avoid any longer.

I do have a current partner, who I have made my aromantic

identity clear to and I've been very open. We have been together for around two years, in an open-solo/poly¹ arrangement. Overall, it is a great relationship, and it has evolved in ways that have made both of us happy. Despite her making me happy, she is a romantic person, and there are always parts of me that will notice or fixate on specific things of our relationship where she wants to be more romantic and I don't. I sometimes have to actively think, 'What would a romantic person do here?' in order to fulfil that. I know she appreciates it, and I know she loves me, and I love her, but I do frequently wonder if it's healthy to be with someone where there is a romantic imbalance. I truly don't know the answer to that.

. . . .

1   Solo polyamory is when someone has multiple relationships but still maintains a 'single' lifestyle.

CHAPTER 4

Aromantic Representation

I can't tell you how proud I am whenever a new piece of media is released with queer main characters. The first homosexual representation I remember seeing growing up was Willow and Tara in *Buffy the Vampire Slayer*, and it fascinated eight-year-old Sam. I honestly think that having that relationship broadcast to me at such a young age really opened my mind to non-hetero love, and I'm so grateful for it. Of course, I'd like to think my upbringing and my other experiences still would've opened my mind later on in life, but I really believe that first kiss between those characters helped shape me from an early age. Since that episode aired in 2001, there has been a plethora of gay and lesbian representation, and I live for all of it. *Love, Simon* brings me to tears every time. *She-Ra and the Princesses of Power* is extremely LGBT+-inclusive and one of my favourite shows of all time. *Heartstopper* is the most adorable thing to grace the television screen. The list goes on.

Unfortunately, the same cannot be said for aromantic representation. Aromantic representation in popular media would solve many of the aro community's visibility issues. Sure, there would still be the erasure and arophobia problems, and there would still be people who don't understand aromanticism as an orientation even if their favourite superhero was aro, but it would put aromanticism on the map, so to speak. With visibility would eventually come acceptance and understanding, and we'd finally have far less explaining to do when a prospective partner or interested party comes along. Imagine someone asking you on a date, and all you'd have to say is 'I'm aromantic' for them to understand why you're turning them down. Representation and visibility could make that a reality.

Of course, aromantic people aren't *completely* invisible; there are some aromantic characters in the media. The main problem with representation is that it's not always positive. Aromantics are often associated with serial killers or heartbreakers, which really isn't ideal. Fortunately, there are also some real, innocent people in the spotlight who manage to give us a good name and prove to the allo masses that we're not evil or heartless.

A-list aros

I'd love to tell you my Google search for famous aros taught me that someone super famous is openly aromantic, but sadly an aromantic person is yet to frequent the Met Gala in an extravagant green, black, white and grey outfit (those and the colours of the aromantic flag, if you weren't aware). However, the aro community does have some good eggs in its midst, surely not limited to the people on this list.

Michaela Coel is a multi-award-winning actress, best

known for her roles in TV shows *Chewing Gum* and *I May Destroy You*. She's also in *Black Panther: Wakanda Forever*, the sequel to Marvel's smash success *Black Panther*, which is a huge win for Team Aro! It's unlikely that she plays an aromantic character, but having aro actors play roles in such a huge franchise is great exposure for the aromantic community. She has only mentioned identifying with aromanticism in one interview with Culture Trip, and is reportedly a very private person, but she did, at least at the time, express an allegiance to Team Aro:

> I Googled aromanticism and I very much felt like, 'Oh, that's me.' Which means if you tell me to dress up nicely because we're going to go to a dinner with candles, it's not going to mean a lot to me. It's a waste of money and I have ingredients at home... I am OK being by myself.[1]

Funnily enough, Coel was enticed to Google aromanticism by an album[2] by our next representative: **Moses Sumney**. The album *Aromanticism* was released in 2017 and received acclaim from several popular news platforms, and songs from the album have featured in many hit TV shows. I actually halted writing this chapter especially listen to *Aromanticism* in its entirety, and although the songs themselves don't scream aromanticism very clearly, there were a few lines in there such as 'We cannot be lovers, 'cause I am the other' and 'If

. . . .

1   Lee, A. (2018) 'Michaela Coel on London and love in Netflix musical "Been So Long".' Culture Trip, 15 November. Accessed on 8/11/2022 at https://theculturetrip.com/europe/united-kingdom/england/london/articles/michaela-coel-i-like-having-intimate-relationships-but-im-ok-being-by-myself

2   Also mentioned in the Culture Trip article referenced in the note above.

lovelessness is godlessness, will you cast me to the wayside? … If my heart is idle, am I doomed? Cradle me so I can see if I'm doomed' that felt quite poignant.[3] According to a *Cultured* article from June 2021, Sumney discovered the term 'aromanticism' while he was writing the album and found that he related: 'With my first album, I felt so dominated by the culture of romance and obsessed with it, even as someone who felt like I was on the periphery of it.'[4] Unfortunately, as with Michaela Coel, there isn't much more information out there about Sumney's orientation.

Alice Oseman is a YA (young adult) author who identifies as aromantic and asexual, and they even wrote a book with an aroace main character. The novel, titled *Loveless*, is about a teenage girl starting university who's desperate for romance but painfully unaware of her aromanticism. The book was released in July 2020, and it's the best aro representation the community could've asked for; it perfectly describes some of the thoughts and feelings experienced by many aro- and ace-spec people – the confusion, the missing sparks, the disgust at being intimately touched – and it does an amazing job at defining aromanticism and asexuality as orientations. I actually read *Loveless* to review for a YouTube video, and honestly I could've highlighted most of the book for quotes. It's such a great tool for anyone who thinks they might identify as aromantic or asexual, and I couldn't recommend it enough. Oseman is openly aroace, and the great thing is that she writes romances – I can't tell you how hard I found it to explain why,

---

3 *Aromanticism*, 2017 album by Moses Sumney. Songs quoted: 'Doomed' and 'Quarrel'.
4 Polachek, C. (2021) 'Moses Sumney on sexuality, 2021 mystery and songwriting.' *Cultured*, 29 June. Accessed on 8/11/2022 at www.culturedmag.com/article/2021/06/29/caroline-polachek-moses-sumney

even when I identified as fully aromantic, I loved romance so much. It's a huge misconception that aromantic people are all completely repulsed by everything romantic – like just because Stephen King writes horror, do you honestly think he enjoys getting stabbed? In a blog interview published in 2020, Oseman said, 'The aro and ace spectrums are so vast, people can have all sorts of different experiences and feelings about things like sex, romance, and intimacy.'[5] *Heartstopper*, a comic created by Oseman, is now a hit Netflix series, and while I'm extremely happy for her and her growing success, I'm also hopeful that with increasing visibility for Oseman and her spectacular work comes increasing visibility for the aromantic community – a *Loveless* film adaptation next, perhaps?

Arguably one of the loudest aromantic advocates, model and aroace activist **Yasmin Benoit** has dedicated all her social media accounts to aromantic and asexual visibility. I actually had the pleasure of meeting Yasmin to interview for a BBC Radio Berkshire documentary she helped to create in July of 2019, and she's broken so much more ground for the A communities since. Yasmin began her work as an activist in 2017, having never felt any romantic or sexual attraction from a young age and later finding her labels, and she's worked with countless established platforms since, including *Attitude*, HuffPost UK, the *Independent*, and Sky News.

Even on YouTube, there don't seem to be many aromantic people. Creators like Lynn Saga and Slice of Ace don't identify as aromantic, although they make helpful and educational content about aromanticism from time to time, but regrettably aros don't seem to get much representation even

. . . .

5   Julia's Bookcase (2020) 'An Interview with Alice Oseman.' Accessed on
    8/11/2022 at https://juliasbookcase.com/blog/alice-oseman-interview

on such a varied platform as YouTube. Unfortunately, having dropped her aro/ace labels and now flailing around in a spiral of confusion, small YouTuber Samantha Aimee (aka me!) is a bit too embarrassed to return to the platform at present. Maybe it'll happen one day, but until then, can some more aromantics please make some content? It would be much appreciated.

Fictional representation

I feel like I barely find any aro rep. I found the show The *Disastrous Life of Saiki K.* on Netflix and I LOVED it. The main character Saiki is definitely aroace; he doesn't understand romance or sex at all. I absolutely loved how the show made fun of romantic relationships and high school dating situations. I was shocked when looking at the Saiki K. fanbase and seeing that other people were not headcanoning him as aroace. The show never explicitly confirms it, but it seems pretty clear in his reluctance to be in a romantic relationship and not understanding romantic attraction.

But besides Saiki K., I haven't seen like any aro rep. I feel that there is so much to be explored with the Split Attraction Model – all the different mixing and matching of labels – and exploring different types of family structures and relationships.

Jenna isn't alone in their frustration. Most of the time, aro representation is speculation; a lot of people have guessed that characters like Dexter Morgan and Sherlock Holmes are aro-spec, but it's been argued that these characters are a negative representation (Dexter being a serial killer and Sherlock being generally heartless) and not quite representation in the first place if their orientations have never been officially confirmed. I've already mentioned Barney Stinson from *How I Met Your Mother*, and although his character eventually becomes more likeable, it still plays into the 'debauched aromantic' stereotype, which isn't a particularly flattering representation.

My own speculations have led me to hope that characters such as Mike Hanlon from Stephen King's *It* and Entrapta from Netflix's *She-Ra and the Princesses of Power* could be aroace. I'm assuming it's not just me who looks for a-spec representation in everything she watches, and I'm sure there's plenty of speculation floating around, but speculation doesn't help the aro community – speculation is probably done solely by aro-spec people and is therefore not going to help spread the word. Aros need confirmation that their favourite characters represent their community, confirmation that alloromantic people can pick up on to raise awareness and education.

One comic book character in particular was portrayed as aro-spec, but TV adaptation *Riverdale* conveniently erased Jughead Jones's identity completely. The *Archie* comics were born in 1942,[6] and Jughead is predominantly portrayed as aroace, preferring to spend his time and money on food. Writer and illustrator Chip Zdarsky even confirmed in a tweet in February 2017 that he 'view[s] him as ace and probably demi-romantic, but for the purposes of his teenage years, aro',[7] but with the predominance of heteronormativity, the *Riverdale* writers just *had* to bow to pressure and make him straight. The first season

. . . .

6   Wikipedia (2022) '*Archie* (comic book).' Accessed on 8/11/2022 at https://en.wikipedia.org/wiki/Archie_(comic_book)

7   Chip Zkarsky, writer and illustrator for the *Archie* comics. https://twitter.com/zdarsky

of *Riverdale* averaged over one million viewers – and the aro community was denied that reach because, unfortunately, sex and romance sell. I personally think Jughead would've been just as popular, if not *more* so, among fans if he was presented as aroace, as he should've been.

Hope does, however, lie within another comic book character: Marvel's own Yelena Belova, super-spy and sister of Black Widow Natasha Romanoff. In 2002, Yelena featured in a miniseries called *Pale Little Spider*, in which she investigated a sex club. Having never grown up surrounded by romance and amatonormativity, the atmosphere is one Yelena isn't comfortable with, and when the madame, Nikki, asks if Yelena is a lesbian, she replies, 'I'm not a lesbian. I'm not... Anything.' In 2020, an article was posted on the Marvel website about the *Black Widow* sisters, and writer Devin Grayson compared the two, stating:

> Nat is older and more experienced and less invested in the approval of others, as well as being a very passionate person who forms deep connections with other people despite the intention not to, whereas Yelena is in some ways less cynical about her ability to change the world than Nat is, less hampered by association with highly principled associates, and probably more likely to identify as asexual than to follow Nat's romantic path.[8]

Despite only the asexual label being used, it's fair to assume

8   Morse, B. (2020) 'Writer Devin Grayson on Natasha Romanoff, Yelena Belova, and the history of "Black Widow".' Marvel, 27 May. Accessed on 8/11/2022 at www.marvel.com/articles/comics/writer-devin-grayson-on-natasha-romanoff-yelena-belova-and-the-history-of-black-widow

from the 'romantic path' part that she's also aromantic. It would be both interesting and invaluable if Marvel were to explore that part of Yelena's character. Although, obviously, the Marvel universe is primarily focused on superpowers and unassailable global threat, just a small, plot-relevant mention would work wonders for aromantic visibility. I know a lot of Marvel fans dislike romance overshadowing the main story, so I think even alloromantic Marvel fans would appreciate a hero rejecting romantic advances and saying, 'Excuse me, sir, I have a world to save.'

Professor Roy Hinkley from the 1960s show *Gilligan's Island* is also blatantly aromantic, even claiming in one episode that he harbours no interest in sex or romance. Russell Johnson, who played the Professor, confirmed that his character was asexual, but I think it's fair to assume that he was also aromantic, rejecting romantic advances and finding much more interest in bugs and flowers.

I wonder how much sooner I'd have discovered aromanticism if there was more than a shred of representation in popular media. Of course, Marvel has been popular for a long time, but just from a brief skim over Google's search results for 'How many people read comics?' I can tell you that far, far fewer people read comics than consume film and television. I've been watching Marvel's adaptations since the first *X-Men* film in 2000, but I think I've only ever read two of their comics, and neither of those featured an aroace spy. Hopefully, with the increasing amount of LGBT+ media, aromanticism will get more than hints or passing mentions in the near future.

How can I represent my community?

How often do you find yourself people-watching? I was doing it today, after I'd finished shopping and I was waiting for my stepmum to leave the shop. From my place on the bench outside, I saw a woman with crutches, someone wearing pink fluffy slippers, someone wearing black shorts and someone with a really cool floaty shirt. That's just off the top of my head, and that was just today. You'd be surprised how many people you notice in your day-to-day life. So what if I'd seen someone wearing a T-shirt with the aromantic flag on it? What if I saw someone whose jumper had 'No thanks, I'm aro' on it? I wonder how many other people would've noticed that T-shirt or jumper today. You take in more than you realize, and you never know who could see an article of clothing like the examples I've given and look up what it means.

The aromantic flag, as I believe I mentioned previously, is comprised of five stripes: two shades of green, a white, a grey and a black stripe. Originally, the aromantic flag consisted of green, yellow, orange and black stripes, but in 2014 it was updated to the current version. The initial colours represented the opposite of romance, friendship, the spectrum between romantic and platonic love, and rejection of traditional romance.

The new flag, whose white stripe was originally yellow to indicate friendship, symbolizes similar things. The two shades of green represent aromanticism as a spectrum, the white stripe represents platonic and aesthetic attraction, the grey represents the grey orientations such as greyromantic or demiromantic, and the black represents the sexuality spectrum. We could leave it at that, but because I'm interested in symbolism, I looked up the objective meaning for each of the colours on the aromantic flag, and this is what I found...

Green is associated with aliens. I read this somewhere and it made me laugh, because although aromantic people aren't little green people from space, they can feel entirely separate from others. Very few people actually understand or empathize with aro-spec people, and many misconceptions circulate about aros that make them feel heavily misunderstood. Green also represents hope, which is a far more positive interpretation – it's nice to think that there's hope for aromantic people to feel the same acceptance everyone else does. Another thing I discovered is that green is the colour of the heart chakra, which, if tapped into, allows a person to love and be loved – another nice association because, as I said, it's a common misconception that aromantic people are unable to love.

White represents purity and innocence – but also coldness. This is quite apt because the most common misconception about aro people is that they're cold-hearted, whereas, in actual fact, aros are generally pure and lovely people. The colour is also incredibly relevant because it contains all the colours of the spectrum – and aromanticism is a spectrum!

Grey is kind of an obvious one: it's the colour used to describe spaces in-between – *grey areas*. It's the colour of neutrality, complexity and compromise.

Black is a colour that represents certainty. One of the most frequently asked questions by alloromantic people to aros is 'How do you know you haven't found the right person yet?' The answer: *you just know*. Black is also achromatic, as are white and grey. As in words like 'asexual' and 'aromantic', the 'a' in achromatic comes from the Greek prefix meaning 'without'

– that is, without colour, which I think is very apt for 60% of the aromantic flag.

Each aro-spec orientation has its own flag, usually featuring some or all of the colours of the default flag. Some aro-spec flags – such as the aroflux, lithromantic and recipromantic (feeling romantic attraction only if the other person feels the same) flags – also contain warm colours like orange and pink to represent romantic attraction, sexuality and the spectrums of attraction. Some aro flags also contain purple, the colour heavily associated with asexuality, which represents community.

But obviously you can't go around wearing an aromantic flag everywhere. Well, you could, but it'd be impractical in some situations – especially if, like me, you work in an establishment that requires you to wear strict uniform. There are many online stores now that offer Pride pins, which I think is a really nice and easy way to show your pride. There's also a wide selection of Pride jewellery online. It's definitely worth looking into; not only will you be spreading awareness in a small way, but you'd also be supporting small businesses!

Other aromantic symbols include griffins (the community's chosen mythical representative, because some people think aromantics aren't real), yellow flowers (to symbolize friendship) and arrows (just because many of us pronounce 'aro' the same way you'd pronounce 'arrow').

Another common symbol coined by the A communities is a ring – a black ring worn on the middle finger of the right hand for asexuality, and a white ring on the middle finger of the left hand for aromanticism. As far as I'm aware, there's no ring that represents being agender, but one Reddit user suggested making grey rings an agender symbol – which finger they'd wear it on is another matter. These rings are more nods to other people in the relevant communities than representation, but you never know what conversation a simple piece of jewellery might strike up:

'Hey, I like your ring!'

'Thanks, it's a symbol of my aromanticism.'

'Oh, what does that mean?'

And so forth. Any little nod to the aromantic community could help spread awareness. Unfortunately, white rings are incredibly hard to come by. I suppose if you're not too picky, a white gold ring could count, but I personally would want it to be *white* white. That's up to the individual, though – I'm assuming not everyone is as picky as I am!

Why is representation important?

Okay, I'm *never* in favour of comparing aromanticism to mental illness because romantic orientation does not equal illness, but we all know one person who insists that depression isn't real, right? An estimated 3–7% of people (depending on what website you look at) have depression, which is between 1.5–3 times more people than those who are aromantic, if you consider my rubbish maths in the introductory chapter to be correct. That means that a minimum of 234 million people have felt the effects of naysayers' erasure. So now, if you're one of the 3–7% of the population who suffers with depression but isn't aromantic, you have an inkling of how an aromantic person feels when someone says something along the lines of, 'But that's not real, you'll find someone eventually.' It doesn't feel nice. So reason number one why representation is important: **erasure reduction**.

For anyone reading this and not falling into either of those percentages – first of all, congratulations on not being depressed! Second, just so you know, being told you're not real is quite the bummer. If we were to increase aromantic visibility and education, far fewer aros would suffer the 'you're not real' rubbish. It makes some people question themselves; since aromanticism is such an unknown thing with so little representation, aros themselves have cause to wonder, '*Am* I making this up?' Answer: no, you're not, and no one has the right to tell you that you are. Other aromantic people, though firm and certain in their identities, might feel saddened, angry or self-conscious if told they're wrong about who they are. It can make you feel embarrassed to tell people about a fundamental part of who you are, and no one wants to hide who they are.

Helping other aromantics realize who they are is another big way representation can help the aromantic community. Imagine growing up, wondering why everyone around you is falling in love and getting into relationships, and never knowing why you're different. Imagine believing people when they tell you you're 'cold' or 'heartless' because you've never been in love, or having people call you a 'slut' for wanting a sexual, non-romantic relationship. Now imagine growing up armed with terminology and a definition for what you are, never having to explain yourself further than simply saying, 'I'm aromantic.' That's a whole chunk of time you've spent unnecessarily wondering who you are, or why you are the way that you are, gone with a simple bit of exposure. That's a whole chunk of time you don't have to spend explaining yourself to Tom, Dick, Harry and everyone else.

Homosexual people suffered through a lot to get to where they are now, and there's still a *lot* of work to be done. But with more representation and education came less homophobia – obviously, I'm not saying homophobia has been completely eradicated because it hasn't, but the gays are arguably closer to equality than ever before. **Arophobia**, though not typically as extreme as the homophobic attacks that have taken place in the past, is sadly quite common, especially online. If you find a *Metro* article or a tweet about how proud someone is to be aromantic, you're sure to find a slew of alloromantic bullies in the comments and replies – some even going as far as threatening corrective rape. Unfortunately, that's the way a lot of people respond when exposed to something they know nothing about: they slate it. It's like when someone is giving you sound logic in a heated argument – if you're unable to argue with their point, you'll often resort to swearing or name-calling. Representation and visibility wouldn't eradicate arophobia straight away, but they could reduce it marginally.

The simplest reason aros need representation is that it would **satisfy their need to be seen**. Relating to the people we see onscreen is the best way to engage with any kind of media. It lets us know we're not weird and we're not alone. It's the sense of pride you get when you see your home town in a popular TV show, or when your workplace is advertised during the breaks between *X Factor* performances. It just feels good to see yourself – even a very small part of yourself – broadcast for the world to see.

Are aromantics LGBT+?

'Are aromantics LGBT+?' is the most searched question on Google regarding aromanticism.

Perhaps one of the reasons aromantic people are so under-represented in the media is that many people don't consider aromantic people to be part of the LGBT+ community, which I suppose is kind of a paradox in itself: if aromantic people are under-represented and overlooked, should they not be part of a movement whose ultimate goal is equality?

According to gatekeepers, the answer is no. Even 22.4% of the aromantic people who partook in the Ace Community Survey of 2014 wouldn't consider themselves LGBT+. I'd be interested to know why, but unfortunately their reasons were not disclosed in the report.[9] Sadly, there are people within the LGBT+ community – and even people who aren't LGBT+ – who are opposed to including anyone who isn't L, G, B or T. 'Why do they need every letter of the alphabet?' I've heard this said on several occasions and I get it – the straights think the queers are building a big army to oppress them as they historically did to us. Dear straights, that is not the aim.

The aim of the LGBT+ community was always equality. Homosexual people want to get married and not be harassed just for loving someone of the same gender. Transgender people want to be accepted for who they are, they want the proper treatment and support, and they too would love to go about their daily lives without being harassed. Non-binary people

9   Siggy (2017) 'Cross-orientations among non-aces.' The Ace Community Survey, Asexual Consensus 2014. Accessed on 8/11/2022 at https://acecommunitysurvey.org/2014/11/17/cross-orientations-among-non-aces

would love it if people would just respect their pronouns. And so on. So with that logic, and the fact that aromantic people just want visibility and for the erasure to stop, why should aros be excluded?

One might argue that much of the LGBT+ community revolves around orientation and that aromantics' feelings aren't oriented anywhere, but not every identity in the LGBT+ community is about orientation. Perhaps the movement used to just be exclusively for homosexual and bisexual people, but it's long since expanded to include different gender roles. From my understanding, the LGBT+ community now welcomes anyone who doesn't identify as heterosexual or cis-gender – heterosexual in this case meaning heteroromantic heterosexual. Of course, there are heterosexual aromantics out there, and you may argue that they're straight enough *not* to be considered LGBT+ – heck, they themselves might not even consider themselves LGBT+ – but at that point I'd argue that it's up to the individual to decide if they want to be a part of the community. Hetero aros are technically still a minority, after all.

So because aromantic people aren't inherently straight, I'd say they're LGBT+. But that's not the only thing that should gain them entry into a club that's supposed to be inclusive: arophobia is also a big issue (which we'll look into further in the next chapter), aromantics are a minority in need of community, and, as is the whole point in this chapter, aros are severely under-represented.

I guess the above is the long answer to the question 'Are aromantics LGBT+?' The short answer: I reckon it's up to you. I personally have been to two Pride festivals dressed to represent the A communities and neither time did I feel left out. No one told me to go home or that I didn't belong there. I was greeted by asexual and aromantic people, and I was complimented on the Pride outfits I'd made. On both occasions, I felt that I was part of the LGBT+ community without a shred of doubt. So if you feel as though you belong, you belong. If you choose not to associate yourself with the LGBT+ community or if you don't feel 'queer enough', that's fine, too. Do what makes you happy.

CHAPTER 5

How to Tackle
Arophobia

The definition of a 'phobia' is 'a debilitating and overwhelming fear of something'. I once had a friend with a vomiting phobia – meaning they were absolutely petrified of throwing up. They experienced crippling anxiety due to this, and they paid a large sum of money to a professional to remedy it. A phobia is an extreme anxiety disorder, if you will. It's for this very reason that I find words like 'homophobic' and 'arophobic' to be both extremely offensive and ironic. The words suggest that the 'arophobic' person is terrified of aromantic people, when in reality the arophobes are the scary ones. Arophobia isn't a clinical mental condition; it's a lack of education and, frankly, brain cells in a person. But alas, the discrimination and harassment of aromantic people is widely referred to as 'arophobia', so I suppose it's the term I'll use.

Discrimination against aromantic people can present itself in a few different forms: institutionalized, internalized and social. It can happen both online and in your day-to-day life, and neither situation is a nice experience. I've explained in detail how representation can minimize arophobia, but unfortunately representation in the media is largely out of our hands, so this chapter is going to delve into the types of arophobia and how best you can tackle them if you come across them.

Types of arophobia

Institutional arophobia isn't really one I've heard a lot about. Institutional discrimination is prejudiced treatment of a certain person or group by an organization, establishment or group of people. A few examples of institutional arophobia could be a landlord opposed to renting out his property to an aro person because they're single and it's just one sole income, or a casting director refusing to hire an aro actor for their romance film because they don't feel romantic attraction. The most common type of institutional arophobia is probably religious. When I requested stories from aromantics across the internet, many of these stories mentioned religion, including Charlotte's:

> I told my mother that I don't want to marry or have children, and while she wasn't mad, she did try to convince me that I have to get married. We're Christian, and marrying in front of the church is part of being Christian.

Lesedi feels similarly and is intimidated by the overwhelming pressure from friends and their religious group to date:

> Now I'm getting older, I know people will expect me to be dating or at least to have dated, which is annoying and a bit

scary. They mostly mean well; they see romance as a natural goal in life, and that romantic pairings are 'God's will', that it's human nature to desire and do these things.

Social arophobia is one of the most common types. Social arophobia is the discrimination against someone by their peers. This includes both online harassment and prejudice from people in real life. I remember sitting in McDonald's with a family friend and telling him I identified as aromantic asexual, and he was very quick to say I just hadn't met the right person. Equally, I've had comments on my online posts – I literally just paused writing this and it took me under a minute to find 'Pray for the right man and enjoy your life' on one of my YouTube videos. I suppose that could count as institutionalized *and* social arophobia.

You'd be surprised by the number of hurtful things people can say to an aromantic person. I posted a tweet recently requesting examples of some arophobic things said to the people of Twitter, and I received many examples, which I'll list below. Be warned, some of the quotes below could be considered quite extreme and potentially triggering.

- Being aromantic is just an excuse to be a sexual predator.
- You're cold and heartless.
- Aromantic people aren't oppressed enough to be queer.
- But you'll be all alone! How can you give up on love?
- That doesn't sound very healthy. You must be mentally sick.
- You just haven't met the right person yet. You'll change your mind some day.
- Maybe you just haven't gone through puberty yet.
- Having a shitty ex isn't an orientation.

- What a waste.
- But you have a girlfriend.
- You're just a lesbian in denial.
- You're going to die alone.
- You're just depressed. You need therapy.

It's quite often that online trolls refer to aromantics as serial killers and narcissists as well. Of course, you can laugh it off because often people don't seek cures for their ignorance and it therefore cannot be helped, but being torn down about a label that gave you answers, peace and a sense of belonging – about something that's a part of you and may never change – is hurtful.

Often praised for her resilience and thick skin when it comes to arophobia, aromantic asexual activist Yasmin Benoit receives more than her fair share of online abuse for her orientations. Across her social media platforms, Benoit sheds light on just how much ignorance and cruelty is thrust upon aromantic people just for being honest about who they are. In a video posted in 2021, Benoit shares an astounding 24 minutes' worth of abusive comments.[1] My personal favourite was '[Aromanticism is] the most twisted and sociopathic of all the made-up orientations'. Although Benoit's responses in the video are generally jokey and light-hearted, I think the response to these remarks is always important – for example, her response to 'Not real. You either didn't find the right person, or something happened to you to place the emotional barrier' was 'You know the right person isn't necessarily

. . . .
1   Yasmin Benoit (2021) 'Reading My Aromantic Hate Comments (Arophobia).' YouTube. Accessed on 8/11/2022 at www.youtube.com/watch?v=PExpoXptmoQ&t=928s

someone you're in a romantic relationship with, right? That is not the epitome of every human relationship', which I think is the perfect way to shut down an arophobic argument and educate someone on just how important different kinds of relationships are. Yes, laughing off arophobia can help you feel better, but it could also help to respond to comments like the above with logic and facts over humour. How else are we going to remedy ignorance?

Comments like those listed above, especially comments such as 'you're just depressed' or 'you're cold and heartless' are arguably a big contributor to **internalized arophobia**. Internalized arophobia is wishing you were different, questioning if you're really who you think you are and wondering if the trolls on the internet are actually right. It comes from within you. Internalized arophobia could look like a lot of things, such as denial. Aromanticism is an incredibly unknown thing, and you know that a lot of people won't understand it and potentially suggest you're a serial killer, right? So in your head, you could say, 'Nope, that's not me. I just haven't found the right person yet. I don't want people thinking I'm a murderer just because I haven't found someone to fancy yet.' Perhaps, as a result, you force yourself into a relationship in the hope that it'll make your life easier, when in fact it just poses different problems for you.

Internalized arophobia can also look like feeling broken or inadequate, low self-esteem, withdrawal from friends and family, shame, depression. No one likes change, be it positive or negative, and many people refuse to accept 'new' information – take old people and smartphones, for example. It doesn't apply to all old people, of course; my granddad is quite attached to his phone, but my grandmother has refused to use a mobile phone since they were first released in 1983.

People just don't like adapting to new information or ideals. Coincidentally, I'm writing this with *Politics Live* on in the background and the panel is discussing gender and trans rights. Transgender people have been around forever, but, for argument's sake, we'll say the terminology originated in the 1950s.[2] By that logic, it has taken 70 years for the trans community to get where they are today, and their rights are *still* being debated. This doesn't exactly instil hope in a community whose terminology only came about approximately 17 years ago. Wide-scale acceptance takes a long time to happen, so why suffer at the hands of arophobes when you could just pretend you're straight?

BECAUSE YOU'RE NOT STRAIGHT, THAT'S WHY.

As Thumbelina's mother so wisely said in the 1994 animated masterpiece *Thumbelina*, 'Never wish to be anything but what you are.' Just because aromantic people are a minority, just because very few people know about or acknowledge aromanticism, it doesn't mean you don't exist and you aren't valid. So what if your neighbour and his mum don't know what aromanticism is? A lot of people don't know what appendicitis is, but that doesn't mean to say I never had it.

Let's talk misconceptions

Naturally, with ignorance come misconceptions. There are a few examples above, among the Twitter quotes, but they only touch the surface. Common misconceptions linked with aromanticism include narcissism, murderous tendencies,

2   Wikipedia (2022) 'Transgender history.' Accessed on 8/11/2022 at https://en.wikipedia.org/wiki/Transgender_history

sociopathy, mental illness, trauma, autism and unattractiveness. Let's break that down.

Narcissism is a personality disorder defined by a sense of self-importance, superiority, strong feelings of envy and a tendency to take advantage of others and expect sympathy. I think people are assuming that aromantics don't feel romantic attraction because they're too busy inflating their own egos and looking down on other people, but that's just not the case. A lot of aromantic people experience internalized arophobia and poor self-esteem, which is arguably the opposite of narcissism.

Often, unfortunately, aromantic people are compared with characters like Dexter Morgan, the main character and serial killer in the TV crime drama *Dexter*, because he doesn't seem to feel romantic or sexual attraction. Such a comparison also leads the simple-minded to believe that other aromantic people must also, therefore, be serial killers. However, as most people with feelings know, nothing is that black and white. If you don't fancy someone, that does not necessarily mean that you want to murder them. That would technically mean I want to murder my entire family. It just doesn't work that way.

Aromantic people are frequently associated by arophobes with sociopaths and psychopaths. Sociopathy, often associated with antisocial personality disorder, is characterized by lack of regard for rules or other people. Similarly, psychopathy symptoms include lack of empathy and faking emotion, but psychopaths are typically less impulsive and angry than sociopaths. According to some people, it's so inconceivable not to feel romantic attraction that you simply must feel no regard for others at all. I'll be the first to admit I know very little about narcissism, sociopathy or psychopathy, but I'm willing to bet that, as with anything misunderstood, there are misconceptions. Common misconceptions surrounding sociopathy, for example, are that sociopaths are emotionless and unlovable. Psychopathy is often mistakenly linked with sadism and, like sociopathy, lack of emotion. I don't know about you, but I'm sensing a theme here. The theme? What we don't understand is cold, heartless and bound to murder us in our sleep.

Many mental illness symptoms seem to include intolerance of or impatience with other people and avoiding contact with loved ones, so obviously those ignorant of the existence of aromanticism and familiar with the symptoms of certain mental illnesses might jump to such a conclusion. One big difference is that many aromantic people thrive in the presence of their loved ones and are very kind and patient. The other difference, clearly, is that aromanticism is a romantic orientation, not a mental condition.

The following section refers to abuse and sexual trauma. Please do not read this part if you think it might affect you negatively – skip to the next section

It's not uncommon for people to assume you've been through some kind of trauma when you come out as aromantic. The debate surrounding this particular misconception divides even the aromantic community itself. Now I want to make it completely transparent that aromanticism doesn't always stem from trauma – most of the time, it's just who you are – but

I do argue that sometimes it *can*. I've publicly said my piece regarding the matter before, and I had several people reach out to me to confirm that, yes, they identify with certain labels because of their trauma. 'My orientation is a result of trauma', one YouTube commenter said. 'I used to love and desire men but after being abused and played I've been left with no desire for anyone. I never want to be touched [romantically] again!' Others commented to the contrary, confessing they'd experienced abuse but did not believe it contributed to their aro orientation. I'm a firm believer in identifying however you feel comfortable, whatever your reasons may be. Orientations can be fluid, and they can be affected by certain people or events. That doesn't make them any less valid. So no, aromanticism doesn't *necessarily* stem from trauma, but it's invalidating to others to argue that it never does.

Recently, a popular mental health advocate boasting more than a million subscribers came out as aroace on their platform, claiming this orientation could've been a result of their trauma. As I said, I believe people are well within their rights to claim certain labels if that's how they feel, but it's both nerve-wracking and hopeful that they associated these two things on their channel – nerve-wracking because they've just told over a million people that their aromanticism could be a result of trauma, which could in theory be the wrong way to introduce an audience to aromanticism, but hopeful because *they told over one million people about aromanticism*. Of course, it's then down to the individual to research aromanticism themselves, but although this person was perfectly valid in what they were saying, it's a little worrying that some people are now going to assume aromanticism stems exclusively from trauma.

End of trauma talk – read on!

Many people assume that because you don't feel romantic attraction, you're autistic. I don't really need to do any research here to debunk this one; I know three autistic people and two of them experience romantic attraction. One of the two is happily married, and the other is very open about her romantic desires, mainly through meme-sharing on Facebook. The third autistic person I can't really speak for, as I don't know them that well, but the two examples I've given are proof enough that many autistic people are alloromantic. Further proof can be found on Netflix's endearing yet ever so slightly patronizing dating show *Love on the Spectrum*, in which autistic people begin their quest for love or the audience follows autistic people already in relationships. Autistic people sometimes have different ways from neurotypical people of showing love and affection, but they have feelings and make strong connections just like everybody else does. It's also a misconception that any disabled aro-spec people are aromantic *because* of their disability, which just isn't the case. It's incredibly ableist to assume that autistic and disabled aros are aromantic because of their differences – and such assumptions most likely stem from the cruel misconceptions that disabled people are unattractive and autistic people don't feel love – both absolutely ridiculous statements. There are autistic aros and there are disabled aros, but that does not mean to say they're aro-spec because of their differences.

I'll keep the final misconception brief because it's utterly ridiculous: 'You're using aromanticism as an excuse not to date because you're just too ugly.' Ideally, I wouldn't give this myth the time of day because it's blatantly incorrect and unnecessarily nasty, but unfortunately it's been said many times to aromantic people. As Chaucer, and later, Shakespeare, famously said, *love is blind*. Beauty is in the eye of the beholder. People fall in love with personality as much as looks, if not more so. Your own looks don't decide your romantic feelings; the prospect is absolutely preposterous.

How do I cope?

With each kind of arophobia, different responses and coping mechanisms may apply. Institutional discrimination is one that needs tackling on a larger scale and often cannot just be laughed off. Trolls on the internet, however, are easier to dismiss. The only wrong way to respond to arophobia is with violence or cruelty. Below I'll provide some examples of responses you can use for different types of arophobia/simple ignorance.

Example #1

Allo: 'You're aromantic? Doesn't that mean you'll be all alone?'
Aro: 'I actually have so many deep and meaningful relationships that I know will last a lifetime. I'm very close with my parents and I have an amazing group of friends.'
Allo: 'But what if your friends get into relationships and forget all about you?'
Aro: 'Some of them already are in relationships. I trust that my bonds with those who aren't in relationships are strong enough that they'll have time for me and any prospective partners; if not, I'll make new friends. You're not

guaranteed a lifetime with anybody, whether they're your partner, a family member or your friend.'

Example #2

Allo: 'Are you sure you're not just depressed?'
Aro: 'Not knowing who I was made me depressed. Finding this label and the community that comes with it has made me feel happy and included.'

Example #3

Allo: 'You just haven't found the right person yet.'
Aro: 'I've found all the right people. My loved ones keep me as fulfilled as I'll ever be.'

Example #4

Allo: 'But aren't you seeing someone?'
Aro: 'The dynamics of the relationship between me and this person are no one else's business, but we have established clear boundaries and I'm very open with them. Sexual relationships don't always have to be romantic.'
Allo: 'So you're stringing them along.'
Aro: 'Not at all. We're honest with each other and we're enjoying ourselves. There's no miscommunication whatsoever.'

In the early stages of our relationship, my partner and I were driving home from Cardiff, and we somehow sparked up a conversation about actor and producer Ryan Reynolds. My partner just could not wrap his head around the fact that I didn't fancy Ryan Reynolds – apparently, it's the law that everyone does – and we ended up having a very long discussion about why I didn't fancy Ryan Reynolds. It was all in good fun and the conversation was light-hearted, but I think I educated him a little bit on how, when I identified as aromantic, those feelings heteronormative society insists everyone has just weren't there. I'd never had crushes on celebrities, and I still don't. I'm not sure he completely understood, but it's good for allos to be open to having these conversations. It's still an alien concept to a lot of people, but the more open-minded people are, and the more willing aromantic people are to be patient and to educate, the better it'll be for aromantic awareness and acceptance.

Tackling internalized arophobia is probably the hardest task. Arguing with yourself and belittling yourself isn't something you can easily just walk away from. Fortunately, there are a few ways you can battle the arophobic demons in your head:

- **Talk to other aro-spec people.** There are aromantic communities all over the internet, and probably physically near you – nearer than you think. Talking to other aromantic people about your shared feelings and experiences will make you feel validated and less alone. Try reaching out on Facebook communities or subreddits, or reach out to someone on Twitter. If you're lucky enough to attend Pride events, make some aro-spec friends. Knowing there are people like you out there will help you feel more sure of yourself.
- **Spend time with your loved ones.** Enjoying the company of the people you cherish will confirm to you that you're fulfilled in your relationships and don't need anything else in your life. You're not missing out; you

have people who enrich your life. Make the most of it and remind yourself that you're loved and important.

- **Reason with yourself.** Coming up with mantras or words of affirmation could help you battle your inner arophobe. Simply reminding yourself that you're not broken, you're perfectly fulfilled and you're great the way you are might not feel effective when you're doing it at first, but the more you tell yourself something, the more you believe it – which I suppose is where internalized arophobia stems from. Fortunately, it works both ways.

  Argue with yourself in the same way you'd argue with any external arophobe. If you're telling yourself you're worthless and alone, for example, respond to that thought. Tell yourself, 'No, I'm loved, and my worth is not defined by who I'm attracted to or what attraction I feel.' Shut down that inner arophobe.

- **Find LGBT+ support.** The Trevor Project is a charity that supports and gives advice to anyone in the LGBT+ community who's struggling. There's even a section on their website on asexuality – unfortunately, nothing about aromanticism just yet, but if you were to reach out, a Trevor Project counsellor wouldn't turn you away. There's the option on their website to call, text or instant message a counsellor if you ever need someone to talk to.[3] Sites like pridecounselling.com also offer counselling for LGBT+ people; however, it may not be affordable for everyone. More on LGBT+ support can be found in Chapter 6.

. . . .

3   www.thetrevorproject.org/get-help

Slut-shaming

> I seriously wish that people would stop slut-shaming allosexual aromantic women and calling allosexual aromantic men 'fuckboys'. I think there are more allosexual aromantics than there are asexual aromantics – but because having sex without romantic ties is frowned upon even in Western societies, a lot of us are 'in the closet'. Especially heterosexual aro women; men can get away easier with casual sex and one-night stands, no matter what their orientation is. The slur 'whore' is really gendered.

> *Anon*

Slut-shaming does just what it says on the tin – belittles people for not conforming to traditional monogamy. Slut-shaming is condemning or punishing someone for dressing provocatively, having multiple sexual partners or one-night stands, or simply acting flirtatiously. It can look like mocking, insulting or even physically assaulting someone for their clothing preference or their actions.

Sexual liberation, although becoming increasingly accepted in modern society, is still more of a dream than a reality at present. The rise of feminism has seen an increase in women's sexual freedom, but there is still a large percentage of people with very traditional, monogamous views who view sexual liberation or experimentation as a negative thing. Traditionally, one person only has sex with another person because they're in love with that person exclusively, and if you have sex with multiple partners without claiming anyone as your one true love, it makes you promiscuous and a terrible person.

The important thing to remember is that there's no one way to be aromantic – and there's no one way to be allosexual aromantic, either. Some allo-aros might still be monogamous with their sexual partner. Some allo-aros may just have one-night stands whenever they fancy. There's nothing wrong with either of those choices. Everyone has the right, aromantic or not, to sexual freedom.

As I've said before, people find change hard to accept. Sex before marriage was frowned upon not so long ago. It took the sexual revolution in the 1960s to bring about acceptance on that issue. Sex with multiple partners, or casual sex, still has a lot of stigma surrounding it, but with fewer people subscribing to the traditional and religious rules and values, and with increased education on polyamory and the right to one's own body, people are slowly starting to come around to the idea of sexual freedom.

Sex is both simple and complicated. Simply put, some people find it fun, and it feels nice, and love is an optional ingredient. However some people find the act very intimate and require a lot of trust to partake in it. Either way, whatever attitude you have towards sex, as long as it's safe, legal and consensual, you should be allowed to have it as often as you please with whomever you please. According to Wikipedia, only 3–9% of mammal species are monogamous[4] – not that I want to compare us to animals, but what I'm getting at is that sex is a natural, instinctual act not always motivated by romance. If people only used sex for its basic intention – to reproduce – we wouldn't be having it anywhere near as much.

---

4   Wikipedia (2022) 'Monogamy in animals.' Accessed on 8/11/2022 at https://en.wikipedia.org/wiki/Monogamy_in_animals

It just so happens that people enjoy it, and they have every right to enjoy it however they want to.

As with the other forms of arophobia, there are different ways to deal with slut-shaming if you're allo-aro. Educating the person is always an option if they're open to it. Reminding them that what you do with your body is really none of their business works, too. For many people, sex is a very personal thing that they don't discuss with others, but if it's something you're comfortable discussing, you should be allowed to do so without judgement. Whatever you decide to do, own it – at the end of the day, other people's opinions really don't matter.

In contrast, asexual aromantics are often referred to as 'frigid' or 'picky'. This can be equally upsetting, but, again, you deserve to exist without judgement. Whatever misconceptions people throw at you, be armed with education and words of affirmation.

Don't let the aphobes get you down.

Misunderstood

A Reddit Submission

[A romance-repulsed aroace has faced much misunderstanding and erasure in school and at home. They fear their parents' reaction if they ever decided to come out, and their school peers don't seem to know or understand how they feel.]

In the mornings, before lessons were due to begin, my best friend and I always sat pretty close to each other. We would sometimes just hug and mentally prepare for the day. In PE, when we had a chance, we sometimes just lay in the grass and cuddled – completely platonic, of course, but since stuff like this is often seen as romantic, I did catch wind of a comment once.

She had her head in my lap during form, and when the bell rang for class, we all got up to leave. But as I was grabbing my stuff, I heard this other (very loud) kid talking about us cuddling all the time. I don't remember the specifics, but I remember him saying something about us being gay.

Well, she's a lesbian. But I'm not – I'm aromantic, asexual and romance-repulsed – so while she didn't mind as much, it kind of got to me.

Another day, she came up to me at lunch and told me that some-one was shipping us. She said she didn't know who, just that someone had told her. I still don't know who it was, but I really hated it. I think it's okay to ship fictional characters, but never real people. Real peo-ple have actual feelings. Some people seem to forget that.

I haven't come out to my parents, because I know they're...let's just say 'strict' about how they think the world should be. They didn't take my older sibling coming out all that well, so I decided to keep quiet, but I've been dropping hints [regarding my opposition to an amatonormative relationship].

I've said so many times before that I don't want to get married and have a family when I'm older (I'm also sex-repulsed), but they told me I'll change my mind when I'm older. When I was little, I wanted to be a famous singer. I've since changed my mind, which is natural, but my parents decided to compare me not wanting a family to me no longer wanting to be a famous singer. [The classic 'you'll change your mind one day/you'll find the right person one day.']

Coming out to friends was scary, too, but thankfully they were as understanding as they could be, so everything ended up fine. And since then it got easier to come out to others.

I recently moved from England all the way to America. My new school has been incredibly accepting (there are so many students with LGBT+ pins, I've seen some with rainbow masks and bags and shoes, too) and I like that I could teach some of my new friends about my orientations! I might be switching schools again soon, so I can only hope they'll be as supportive as my past schools.

[Although the parents and the school peers weren't inherently unkind in the story, even the assumptions that the protagonist was homo-sexual or would one day change their mind about their orientation could've caused them to feel invalidated or embarrassed. Although no harm might've been meant, such comments could even cause internalized arophobia in the person.

It's incredibly hard, sometimes impossible, not to feel invalidated when so few people know about aromanticism. At some point someone will say something potentially damaging without even meaning it. On those occasions, try to be patient with the person. Maybe try to educate them if they're open to it, or simply just remind yourself that you *are* valid and you don't need fixing.]

CHAPTER 6

Aromanticism and Mental Health

Please bear in mind that this chapter will deal with mental illness, and therefore may contain mention of depression, anxiety, self-harm and other sensitive topics. Anyone with any mental health concerns should seek help from a medical professional. I am unqualified to give medical advice and can only draw from my own experiences.

Helplines will be listed at the back of the book.

This right here is why I don't want to believe I'm not completely aromantic. Say I developed a bond with someone and then romantic feelings came into play. Romantic attraction presents itself to me so rarely that it feels sacred and special and intense, and I don't know what I'd do if the person rejected me. I'm consumed with thoughts of this person, and I feel miserable when they're not talking to me and I make myself miserable thinking they obviously don't like me back. I can't just hop on Tinder and find a new person to be attracted to.

What it boils down to is that I'm quite miserable. I wanted to hurt myself the other night. I just couldn't be bothered.

An entry from my journal, August 2020

Basically, I'm miserable again because my sister is in a relationship and my best friend is in a relationship and I'm just really insignificant. What is even the point in me? Just to be here when I'm needed and cease to exist the rest of the time? No one would notice if I stopped making videos. Nothing I do matters, and nothing I do will ever matter.

I have no one to share things with.

I don't like how I look a lot of the time.

I'm nobody's priority. I could prioritize myself, but even I don't like me that much.

Journal entry, July 2021

FOR DATING:

You can't be a shut-in forever

Scared of being pathetic and alone

I've never dumped anyone before and I'm scared/unsure how.

AGAINST DATING:

Expensive

You don't really care

I'm not sure what I want

He's super into kissing you and sometimes you just don't want to kiss him

You like being pathetic and alone.

Journal entry, January 2018

In spite of the journal entries above, I usually considered being on the aromantic spectrum a positive thing. I was happy having that definition of who I was, and I was happy with the relationships I had. Sometimes, however, the constant normalization of a traditional romantic relationship being forced down your throat when you know in your soul it's not meant for you...well, it can get to you. Just please know that if you've ever felt the way I felt when I was struggling with my identity, the negative thoughts are always wrong. I always had people to share things with, I was never alone, and I was never pathetic. The same goes for you. We don't like to think our aromanticism can be the cause of our sadness. Society's response to aromanticism and, consequentially, internalized arophobia are more likely the cause of the sadness. We've got enough people assuming aro-spec people are all miserable and loveless, so confirming that our lack of romantic attraction might make us sad sometimes gives credit to the arophobes. But the aromantic community is a misunderstood minority, and until the wider population understands aromanticism a bit better, there are going to be aspects of our orientation that might get us down sometimes. I used to get depressed because my ears stick out – that doesn't mean to say they're not a part of me and I'm going to chop them off. It's the same with your orientation – whatever minority you're part of, I guarantee that once upon a time you thought about how much easier life would be if you were just straight and/or cisgender, but your orientation was and will always be a part of you. One day, people will accept that aro-spec people are just as 'normal' as everyone else and we'll all be a bit less sad.

One day, sometime between 2013 and 2015, I spent the entire day sitting on the sofa crying. My mum and sister were at work, and I had the house to myself all day. I had plans later that day to go and see one of the *Hunger Games* films in the cinema with a guy – I believe I referred to him as Chester in Chapter 3.

He was a regular customer in the post office where I worked, and he looked like Jason Momoa. There were certain things about him that I was uncertain about, like the fact that he smoked and he had kids, but he was a human person with romantic interest in me. Did it matter that I didn't reciprocate those feelings? Nah, they'd come with time, right? He was willing to watch a sequel to a film he hadn't even seen to spend time with me, so that was nice, wasn't it?

Only, the day came and I felt sheer panic. Every single part of me was screaming *no*. I'd never felt anxiety like it; I couldn't get changed out of my dressing gown, I couldn't move off the sofa, I couldn't get a single thing done. Time was ticking closer to our meeting, and I knew I couldn't do it. I cancelled, and the relief came instantly, albeit accompanied by guilt. The depression, however, didn't subside completely. I was desperately lonely and terribly confused. Why couldn't I just date like a 'normal' person? If I pushed Chester away, who would love me?

Depression doesn't always need a cause. I've spent long periods of my life being depressed, sometimes with reason, sometimes without. Unfortunately, my perpetual singleness and what I thought was extreme pickiness was occasionally the cause of my low moods. Aromanticism being so unknown can be an issue for aromantics themselves; I've lost count of the number of times I thought I was weird or had a piece missing, and that can really impact someone's mental health. This is a big reason why visibility is such an important thing for aro-spec people. However, some people just happen to be mentally ill *and* aromantic, and the two don't necessarily overlap.

Forcing yourself to date when you know fundamentally that you don't want to will not help you. I felt wrong in many of my past relationships, but I pushed it and it never ended well. I'd go on a perfect date with a lovely person, kiss them, come home, and wonder why I felt so uncomfortable. I'd get along well with someone, and all the pieces will have fallen into place, but when they leaned in to kiss me, the pieces all came apart. Because of these experiences, I was very miserable and confused, and it took me a lot of tears, Googling and Tinder scrolling before I made peace with maybe never being in a relationship again. I made that peace, and then I met someone who stirred up feelings in me I'd assumed I'd never feel – which knocked me for six all over again.

I believe romance is such a trigger for depression, whether you're romantically inclined or not. Think about how many scenarios linked to romance can cause depression or anxiety: breakups, fear of them cheating/leaving, feeling sad when your significant other is busy, rejection, feeling insecure or not attractive enough for your partner, inability to find a partner, jealousy (rational or irrational)... The list goes on. According to *The Wall Street Journal*, recent studies have concluded that being in love can actually make changes in your brain similar to drug addiction and obsessive-compulsive disorder (OCD).[1] And because romance is so normalized, apparently aromantics are weird and broken if they don't want all that drama. Go figure.

With all this in mind, we can pinpoint three different causes for low moods: loneliness, romance and other. This

. . . .

[1] Parker-Pope, T. (2007) 'Is it love or mental illness? They're closer than you think.' *The Wall Street Journal*, 13 February. Accessed on 8/11/2022 at www.wsj.com/articles/SB117131067930406235

concludes that aromanticism *can* be a cause of sadness, but it isn't always. The important thing to note at this point is that it doesn't make you a 'bad aromantic'; no one in the community is going to spite you for how your identity makes you feel.

When I first tried to come out as aromantic and asexual to some of my friends, they said, 'So... You mean you are gay, right?' That's when I realized aroace representation wasn't as prevalent as I thought. I went into a negative spiral. I went back to thinking I was broken. Funny thing is, I tried dating one of the friends I told and he cheated on me because I couldn't provide the things he wanted. He wanted someone who was willing to do physical things. After that relationship ended, I didn't date anyone. It wasn't that I didn't want to date people, it was more that I couldn't make myself pretend to be normal.

Anon

I started experiencing alienation from my friends when I came out as aromantic. They saw me as pretentious or as if I thought I was morally superior just because I didn't have crushes or experience intense feelings toward certain 'desirable' class-mates. I knew I had to figure out a way to reconnect and not lose my space within my tribe of friends – we were already the weird arty kids, and I couldn't afford to lose even them. I didn't realize it until much later that my motivations were social acceptance, nor did I realize that what I ended up doing is called masking.

Billie[2]

. . . .

2   This name is not the person's real name.

I wish I could say that once I found out that romantic feelings were something I don't really have, I fully embraced it and lived happily ever after. That really couldn't be farther from the truth. That's not to say I'm unhappy or miserable in my relationships, but there has been a lack of an embrace of my aromantic self that I can't truly bring myself to change. There will always be a part of me that feels as though I'm broken.

The part of it that really kills me is that I don't feel broken from a perspective of making myself happy, I feel it from the perspective of letting others down. I love building connections, making friends, partners and relationships. I truly and fully embrace relationship anarchy (the rejection of amatonormativity), but every person that comes into my life will form a different bond with me, and that bond can last two weeks or two years, and still be special.

However, it kills me inside when I make a connection with someone, and even if they are fully okay with me being solo-poly or non-monogamous, they start to develop romantic feelings, and then I have to reject them. I feel as though I am somehow letting them down, like there is a part of me that should be romantic back, but I just cannot bring myself to do it, as though wanting it enough will fix it.

C.D.

Surrounding yourself with open-minded and understanding people is fundamental for accepting your identity and feeling safe enough to be open about it. Finding the terminology to explain who you are can fill you with so much confidence, but that confidence can shatter with the smallest comment from people you care about. Remember there are multiple ways you can find someone to talk to; invisible as aromantics are at present, they're everywhere, and the community is there to help you.

Friends are sometimes hard to come by, and losing your circle of friends is a scary thought, but you need to make sure you have friends who accept you. Are they really your friends if they refuse to understand you? Being accepted by peers is something everyone wants, but if it means changing who you are or masking (hiding who you are to conform to social pressures or protect yourself from possible harassment), it really isn't worth it sometimes.

An overlap

Mental illness and romantic orientation aren't always linked but can occasionally overlap due to lack of education – if you've never heard of aromanticism, certain feelings or experiences can be mistaken for romantic attraction. Reddit user take-to-the-highways is diagnosed with borderline personality disorder (BPD) and OCD, and it took a long time for them to realize they were aromantic, having confused hyperfixation with romantic attraction:

> I recently came to terms with the fact that I'm aromantic, but it took me a long time to realize because I have BPD and OCD, and when my mental illness got bad, I would hyperfixate on someone and I always interpreted it as a 'crush'. I had dreams about dating them, I would fantasize about it and everything, but whenever I actually dated someone or thought about asking my 'favourite person' out, I just felt so severely uncomfortable about it.
>
> I recently got diagnosed with BPD and came across the

term 'favourite person' and everything clicked into place. [After] all these years of me trying to enter relationships just because it was 'normal', putting myself into situations that made me so uncomfortable that I would have panic attacks, cursing myself because I couldn't just be happy or even content in a relationship...I felt like a pressure had been released off of me.[3]

Take-to-the-highways also commented that their cravings for physical touch were often confused for romantic feelings. Since this post, the Reddit user has entered into a relationship but still identifies as 'aromantic with an exception', which was nice to hear as I've used similar terms myself in the past.

Another aromantic person with BPD commented on the original post that they experienced something similar regarding hyperfixation, stating they thought they'd been in love before but it actually turned out to be idealization and obsession. Many people with BPD have a 'favourite person', someone they have such an intense attachment to that they feel they cannot live without them. These feelings can be characterized by extreme attachment, willingness to move countries or cities to be with this person, craving attention from this person, feeling jealous and being eager to please them. People with BPD who feel romantic attraction might make their significant other their 'favourite person', but for an aromantic person with BPD, this fixation on a particular person could be confused for romantic attraction and might make it hard for them to figure out their romantic orientation. Some people

. . . .

3   Original post by take-to-the-highways, quoted with permission of the user: www.reddit.com/r/aromantic/comments/erk9na/ aromanticism_and_mental_illness

with BPD found that therapy helped them manage these intense feelings and better figure themselves out.

Sam the agony aunt

I was both surprised and unsurprised by how many people on the internet speculate over whether they're aromantic *or* depressed. I've seen a few posts online from people who used to feel romantic attraction but, since developing depression, no longer feel romantic attraction. As I've mentioned before, depression and other mental illnesses can dull your emotions and lower any desire you might feel for someone, and your depression may well be making you 'feel aromantic'. It's not ideal for anyone to confuse aromanticism with depression, but sometimes feelings get tangled and that's okay. The way I see it is if you feel that you're aromantic, you can identify that way. Romantic orientation isn't always permanent, and it makes some kind of sense that your mental state could affect your levels of attraction. However, it's always important to note that just because some people blame trauma or mental illness for their lack of attraction, it doesn't mean the same for all aromantics. Not everyone's romantic orientation is fluid, and a lot of aromantic people lack romantic attraction every single day of their lives without cause or change.

I was initially going to take to Twitter and ask people to tell me their problems, but it felt a bit obnoxious, so I've created a few fictional scenarios below that some aro-spec people might relate to and I came up with some advice. I know that's still a bit obnoxious, but I hope it helps anyone who struggles with their aro identity.

> I'm aroflux and in a relationship, and I'm worried that because my orientation fluctuates, I'm just going to stop loving my partner all of a sudden.

There are two different definitions of aroflux: those who fluctuate between alloromanticism and aromanticism, and those who fluctuate on the aromantic spectrum exclusively. People fluctuate at varying degrees over varying timescales, under many different circumstances. For me, when I explored the aroflux label, if I ever felt romantic attraction for someone and developed a romantic bond, it wouldn't ever disappear. Of course, it's different for everyone and your fears are valid, but whether your romantic attraction comes and goes or not, you're still able to love your person. If you're honest and open with them from the start, they'll know what to expect, and they'll know that just because your romantic feelings might fade and return now and then, it doesn't mean you don't love them in other ways. Trust yourself and trust your partner.

> All my friends are in relationships, and I'm left out of social gatherings sometimes because they like to go on double dates or romantic outings. I feel like I should find a partner just to fit in with my friends, but I know I don't want one. It's really getting me down.

I'm going to use the old 'if all your friends jumped off a bridge' scenario here – I know it's a tired one, but it's relevant. If all my friends jumped off a bridge, I'd understandably be very sad, but I'd like to think I'm sound enough of mind not to do so myself. It would take time and grieving to build connections with new people and bring back some sort of equilibrium, but there is always something to live for.

So why would you consider stringing some poor soul along just to fit in with your friends? In all likelihood, forcing yourself into a relationship you don't want would make you even more miserable – and you'd be hurting someone else in the process. My advice would be to find some new friends. Don't lose touch with your old ones, of course, but maybe join a local LGBT+ group or volunteer somewhere to meet new people. Your real friends will always make time for you, but it never hurts to connect with new people.

Alternatively, find some solo hobbies. I'm quite terrible at making new friends, so if I were to read the above advice in a book, I wouldn't take it. Hobbies, on the other hand, are something you don't need companions to enjoy. Take up knitting, pottery, painting, writing or crochet. Creating something with your own two hands can fill you with such a sense of accomplishment, and when your friends make time for you, you can gift them with a cute little pot you sculpted – a reminder of what a great and talented friend you are.

Fear of losing your loved ones is universal – everyone feels it. But try to remember that your friends love you, whether they're in relationships or not. A lot of the time, being the only one in a friendship to set up plans can be annoying, and you can end up refusing to make plans out of spite. Try to be adult about it: if you've planned something with your friends and you have a great time, the planning was worth it. Be proud of what a good friend you are.

I'm friends with a guy and I love him so much platonically, but I'm really scared he's going to want more. He's my best friend and I don't want to lose him, but I can't reciprocate any romantic feelings he might develop.

I've been here before: being so careful with what you say so you don't lead anyone on, making it clear you're not romantically available, and somehow you're still unable to prevent the other person catching feelings. It's no one's fault, but it can ruin a perfectly good friendship when one side develops romantic feelings the other doesn't reciprocate. It can make you too anxious to even open notifications from others in case the person notices you're online. It can make you scared to face them.

Unfortunately, the only thing you can do in this case is make your boundaries abundantly clear. Maybe if they're hinting that they're looking for a relationship, you can offer to be their wing person – scroll through dating apps with them, go out with them to meet new people, let them know how hopeful you are that they'll find an amazing person who will love them in the way they deserve. Maybe start calling them super-platonic names like 'bro' or 'mate'. These aren't foolproof – my partner calls me 'mun' and 'mate' quite regularly – but it's worth trying just as a subtle hint.

But while you're making it clear you don't feel romantically inclined towards them, also make it clear that they're important to you. Your main worry is losing your friend, so make sure they know you care. Let them know you're worried you'll lose them to unreciprocated romantic feelings. It's an awkward conversation to have, but the more truthful you are, the easier your life will be.

> I feel worthless and unloved because I'm not in a relationship. I'm scared everyone will forget about me.

I think my main problem when I had this mindset was tunnel vision. A lot of people really undervalue the importance of family – probably because it's such a common goal for people to move out of their parents' house, and because it's so natural to fly the nest, but whether you have those ambitions or not, it doesn't mean your family shouldn't still be important to you. When I wrote the journal entries at the beginning of this chapter, I was thinking about my friends and my sister – people my own age. Looking back at them now, my mother was the first person I thought of. I wonder how she would've felt if she'd known I was feeling that way back then. My mum has always been in my life, and she's always been there for me to talk to. Our views don't always align, but she's only ever wanted me to be happy – and she's not the only person I disregarded when I wrote those words.

My dad gives the best hugs and he's my favourite person to cry on. My nan is a great person to vent to and she never judges me. I have this big, loving family who will always be there for me no matter who else comes and goes, and I hate that I ever took them for granted. I know in reality that my friends and my sister will never forget about me, but if I ever feel those fears, I need to start reminding myself that they're not the only people in my life.

There will always be people in your life that you're important to, whether you remember that all the time or not. You're too important to forget.

No one understands when I tell them I'm aromantic, so I've stopped telling people, but now I just feel alone and closeted, like I can't fully be myself. What should I do?

Sometimes, I'm ashamed to admit, I would take the easy way when anyone asked me if I was seeing anyone. I'd simply say,

'Nah, I'm not interested in dating', or something along those lines. That way, I never had to explain myself any further to the person because those words are easily understood. However, in shutting down the conversation that way, you're not allowing the person to even attempt to understand you fully. It's a difficult conversation to have, but telling someone you're aro-spec is a necessary conversation to have. Just by being honest and open with people, whether they understand or not, you're increasing aromantic awareness. Even if you just tell one person, maybe it'll snowball. The conversation might spark a thought in the person's brain: 'Oh, maybe that's what my sister is – she doesn't seem interested in dating at all. Maybe I should ask her if she's heard of it.' Or maybe it'll just begin conversations between other people: 'Did you know Susan's aromantic? I never knew what it was, but she explained it means she doesn't feel romantic attraction.' You never know what effect your courage and honesty might have.

Of course, I understand that people's lack of understanding can bring you down, but it's just a case of validating yourself and remembering that you're *you* and you're irreplaceable, and your identity cannot be changed or argued away. It doesn't matter that your nan doesn't get it when you tell her why you're never getting married; she loves you either way, and whether you have a partner or not really doesn't affect her life.

With repeated reminders to people who ask you why you're not dating, you're drilling 'I'm aromantic' into their brains, however slowly, and one day they'll finally understand. Be strong and be firm. If someone pokes fun or insists you're wrong, they don't belong in your life anyway. You deserve people who attempt to understand you, people who accept you for who you are. Sometimes it can be hard to be yourself, but you are the only guaranteed constant in your own life. Don't compromise that.

> I want a relationship so badly, but I know I'll never feel romantic feelings. I feel like I'm missing out, and I'm finding it really hard to come to terms with.

I've already gone into depth about all the types of relationships you can get into as an aromantic person. Unfortunately, I've seen many accounts from people who feel this way, so you're not alone if you do, too. I've been in several relationships fuelled on my part by wishful thinking that they'd make me 'normal', and although I cared very much for those partners, my romantic attraction to them was often limited or not there at all. I was in denial before I even knew the word for what I was. The irony is that when I tried to force relationships because I wanted one so badly, they never worked, but when I finally accepted that I probably wouldn't ever find an amatonormative relationship and was happy with that fact, I found one. Life has ways of surprising you, and whether your orientation is fluid or not, you'll find your happiness somewhere. Maybe that happiness won't come in the shape of a person – maybe you'll find an amazing job that makes you feel as if your life has come together, or maybe you'll backpack around Europe and realize that your happiness comes from within yourself.

Romance isn't the be-all and end-all of existence, and as tragic as it might feel to you right now, I promise it won't always feel that way. Whenever I craved some sort of connection with someone, I found writing romantic fiction always soothed me. It was a fictional romance, yes, but it was a relationship I'd created with all the elements I could imagine or want. It's weird to say, but there are many things that feel like being in love: singing along to sad Taylor Swift songs, writing fiction, watching romantic films, riding in the back of your best friend's car between two of the people you're closest to with the windows down and the music on loud, being greeted by your dog when you get home... So many moments in your life are going to make you feel so full. Hold on to that truth when you're feeling low, because those moments are worth everything.

Where to get help

> In the end, I keep feeling torn between not feeling romantic attraction and feeling sadness for missing out on what a romantic relationship has to offer. I don't want to feel broken. I'm just so torn about this all the time that I end up getting depressed.
>
> *Reddit post on r/aromantic, January 2021[4]*

A study involving 1023 aro-spec people in August 2020 provided worrying results regarding the mental health of aromantic people. Obviously, a thousand people is a small percentage of the aromantic population as a whole. Even so, this study found that 71% of the people involved in the survey had thought about suicide and 17% had even attempted it; 72% believed that their aro-spec identity and their depression could be related, and an even higher percentage of people

. . . .

4   Reddit post: www.reddit.com/r/aromantic/comments/ko768s/ does_anyone_else_feel_depressed_about_being

reported they felt alienated by their loved ones because of their identity.[5]

The world as it is right now does not cater for aromantic people. Under-representation, misconception, ignorance and amatonormativity make existing as an aro-spec person very difficult. We know how we can tackle these issues, but the battle is going to be a long one, as every LGBT+ battle has been and continues to be. In the meantime, roughly seven in ten aromantic people (according to the August 2020 survey) are considering taking their lives. So how can we tackle identity-related low mood while so many people remain ignorant?

LGBT+ charities

I mentioned the Trevor Project in the previous chapter. I've never utilized their service before, but I've heard many good things about this charity. The Trevor Project website offers counselling, suicide prevention information and advice on sexual health. Stonewall is another LGBT+ charity that has recently started shedding light on aromanticism, and on their website you can find lots of help and advice, including a helpline that's open on weekdays. Switchboard is a helpline for LGBT+ people whose website offers many ways to reach out to talk.

You can even reach out to charities that aren't LGBT+-exclusive: the Samaritans, Papyrus UK Suicide Prevention or the National Suicide Prevention Helpline UK. I'll list the contact details for each charity here:

. . . .

5   'Mental health and suicidal tendencies within the Aromantic-spectrum.' Accessed on 11/11/2022 at https://docs.google.com/document/d/1SahjBFcdf7qNgV85wXz3jUP9ILQyuk8olKdFIbefe4I/edit#

- **The Trevor Project:** www.thetrevorproject.org
- **Stonewall:** www.stonewall.org.uk, 0800 0502020
- **Switchboard:** https://switchboard.lgbt, 0300 330 0630
- **Samaritans:** www.samaritans.org, 116123
- **Papyrus UK:** www.papyrus-uk.org, 0800 068 4141
- **National Suicide Prevention Helpline UK:** 0800 689 5652
- **National Suicide Prevention Lifeline (USA):** 1-800-273-8255
- **LGBT Youthline (Canada):** 1-800-268-9688
- **Lifeline (Australia):** 13 11 14
- Other/international helplines and websites are listed in the back of the book.

Therapy

Counselling or therapy is a privilege not everyone can afford, but if you're fortunate enough to have access, it can be a massive help. Free NHS counselling is available in the UK – however, you should probably expect a hefty waiting list. Costs for private counselling can range from £30 to £70 per session; some practices offer discounted prices to students or people on low incomes. If you can, make sure your therapist is LGBT+-friendly – look on their website to see if anything is mentioned, because the more understanding and sympathetic your healthcare professional is, the better you'll feel. If you're at school, it's entirely likely that your school also offers counselling. Ask a trusted teacher or member of staff for details. Therapy prices are between $65 and $250 in the US, and somewhere between $60 and $180 in Australia. For a lot of people, this is unaffordable, but that's where helplines and charities could come in useful for you.

Friends/family/other trusted confidants

Talking to those you know well is often harder than talking to a professional or a stranger, simply because if you don't know the person, their judgement matters way less to you. But if you have a friend or family member that you can trust, talk to them. You won't be burdening your loved ones with your problems; they want you to be happy and they more than likely want to help.

If you're uncomfortable talking to someone you're close to about your mental health, consider the other people in your life: teachers, a friendly colleague or your manager at work perhaps. Don't be silent. There is always someone who will listen.

AROMANTICISM IS NOT A DISORDER

Personally I felt uncomfortable [talking about my aromanti-cism] because my therapist never understood the concept. I talked about my 'special someone' and they never grasped that it was not romantic or sexual even after I explained it. They told me I'd eventually fall in love with someone.

@saltyypotatoh on Twitter

Another huge issue with lacking aro visibility is uninformed healthcare professionals. Ever since I discovered the term 'aromantic', I have come across so many accounts of people having gone to therapy and being told by their counsellor that their lack of attraction was 'disordered'. So many mental illnesses and even physical illnesses can dull your drive for romance and sex, and as I mentioned before, it's a big misconception that aromantic people are just mentally ill or broken. Medical professionals know the symptoms of mental illness, and because aromanticism is so unknown, these professionals use the only knowledge they have: that mental illness is often the cause of lack of romantic interest. Aromantic people get put on antidepressants, and yet the romantic attraction doesn't magically materialize. They're just a bit less depressed, but still sad that no one really understands them. It's not necessarily the medical professional's fault they've never heard of aromanticism, but it sure doesn't help. As AUREA so brilliantly puts it: 'How can we get help when the people we need are those with the tools to undermine us?'[6]

Often therapists can focus on *why* you don't feel romantic attraction, as if that's the thing that needs fixing, when in fact the thing you need to focus on is finding fulfilment in other aspects of your life. Many aro accounts report that therapists have told them to 'put themselves out there', which seems to me like overstepping. Even with counselling, there should be a boundary; for many allo people with mental illnesses, advising even them to date when they're mentally ill could be dangerous. In my admittedly limited experience, the best kind of counsellor will ask you to look within yourself or ask you open questions, because even though they're the professional, often the patient knows what's best deep down and they just need that little nudge to realize it.

Lack of knowledge on the aromantic spectrum in medical professionals is especially dangerous because they could incorrectly diagnose their patient with mental or physical illness to explain the lack of attraction. This could result in

. . . .

6   AUREA (2021) 'Finding a therapist as an aromantic.' Accessed on 11/11/2022 at www.aromanticism.org/en/news-feed/finding-a-ther-apist-as-an-aromantic – definitely worth a read if you're an aro-spec person with mental health issues.

hormone therapy, medication or talking therapy, which in itself could be a subtle kind of conversion therapy. We know the distinction between romantic orientation and mental conditions, but unfortunately the people who matter don't, and I'm going to say it again: *this is why education and visibility are so important.* Aromantic people who struggle with depression or other mental illnesses deserve professionals who understand and support them properly.

CHAPTER 7

How to Be an Ally

You've surrounded yourself with good people. You have an amazing family and a close group of friends. These people only want what's best for you, but unless you identify as aromantic yourself, aromanticism can be a difficult and complex thing to understand. People are going to say the wrong thing, no matter how much they love you, so this chapter is a tribute to those people. They're trying.

Allos supporting aros

Okay, so you're an alloromantic person with an aromantic friend. Maybe they've only just come out to you, and although you're supportive, you have no clue about aromanticism or how you can support your loved one.

How can you give comfort if your aromantic friend is struggling? Are you allowed to point out the smoking-hot lad across the road and profess your love at first sight, or is that insensitive? How do you let your loved one know that you're available to help however you can and that you're there for them?

Here are a few ways that you can be not only a friend, but an ally also:

- **Be open-minded.** Aromanticism is a spectrum, and in all likelihood, your aromantic friend feels a very specific way about certain things. Just listen to what they tell you and accept it as fact. It's how they feel, and it doesn't hurt you in the slightest. Yes, you might be confused by what they're telling you, but be patient and try to understand where they're coming from. Just because you may not have heard of this before, it doesn't make it fiction.

- **Love them!** Your friend might not feel romantic attraction at all, or they might feel romantic attraction under certain circumstances – either scenario could mean that they're likely to not want or not have a partner. This makes you, their friend, all the more important to them. Set up friend dates – go to the cinema, have a picnic in the park, pick strawberries. Make sure they know they're just as important to you as you are to them, whether you have a partner or not. If people put enough effort into their friendships, maybe romance would be knocked off its pedestal a little bit.

- **Do your own research.** There's a slowly increasing amount of information on aromanticism out there. Sites like Reddit and Twitter are popular platforms for aromantic people to share their experiences, as well as video-sharing sites such as YouTube and, more recently, TikTok. I'll list some helpful sources and creators at the end of the book, but searching 'aromantic' on any one of those platforms is bound to get you started.

It could also help to research arophobia and discrimination surrounding aromanticism, and figure out how you can better support aros as a whole. Find out what to say and what not to say to and about aro-spec people.

- **Ask questions.** As helpful as social media and search engines may be, you will not find all the knowledge and answers there. Your aro-spec pal will be more than happy to talk to you about their experiences as long as you go by the first two bullet points: be open-minded and show them you care. No two aromantic people are the same, which makes aromanticism difficult to understand as an outsider, but the more you ask, the more you'll know. I can't tell you how difficult I've found trying to explain aromanticism to someone, no matter how understanding they try to be, but the important part is being patient with each other.

- **Include them.** If you're in a relationship yourself, you might find that your priorities are different from those of your aromantic friend. According to popular belief, no one likes being a third wheel, right? But is that *really* right? I've always been more than happy to spend time with my sister and any partners she's had, and when I visit my friend, I stay in the house she lives in with her partner. I have no difficulty enjoying their company, be it with them alone or them and their partners. So what if they hold hands every now and then? Other people's affection towards each other shouldn't make the so-called 'third wheel' feel uncomfortable – unless the couple in question is partaking in a game of tonsil tennis, of course. Being surrounded by affection should only ever be a positive thing. I'm not saying you have to take your aromantic friend out on all your dates and do away with valued alone time with your partner, but it doesn't hurt to invite them shopping as a threesome or ask them to tag along for a cinema trip. I guess it depends on the person, but I'm sure many aro-spec people would be happy to spend time with their friend, third-wheeling it or not. Of course, you don't always have to bring your partner along either; go out for some one-on-one time with your aro friend as well.

- **No outing!** Understandably, coming out as aromantic to someone can be quite uncomfortable, especially if they're unwilling to understand your explanation, so please be mindful that your aromantic friend might've deemed you special enough to be the *only* person they've come out to. Don't assume they're comfortable with everyone knowing their label. It's not nice for anyone of any orientation to be thrust under a spotlight by their peers, whether it's malicious or not. If romance crops up in conversation with a third party, let the aromantic person be the one to bring up their orientation, and until that happens, just talk about your own experiences.

Also, to answer the above question 'Can I point out the smoking-hot guy across the road to my aromantic friend?' – yes, absolutely! Aromantic people understand when someone is good-looking; in all likelihood, they're admiring the guy, too. Aesthetic attraction is when you find someone attractive to the eye, so by all means point out people who you think look nice. The aromantic person might not be looking at him in the same way as you are, but that's okay. Don't objectify the hot guy, obviously, but it never hurts to appreciate from afar!

Aros supporting allos

As well as aromantics feeling out of the loop, alloromantic people also need certain kinds of patience and support from their aromantic friends. It's possible your allo friends might be made to feel guilty or misunderstood by you as an aro, so it's important that you're there for your allo peers as much as they are for you.

Here are some simple ways you can make your alloromantic pals feel loved:

- **Be happy for them.** It's understandable that you might feel lonely, scared or betrayed if your allo friend enters into a relationship, but it's important to remember that their needs are just as important as yours, however different. Try to consider your friend's partner as another friend as opposed to competition for their attention. Your allo friend would be happy for you if you were to find a queerplatonic partner, and however anxious you feel about losing them, you should treat them the same.
- **Include their partner.** As much as you may want your friend to yourself sometimes, it could really make them feel loved and considered if you invite their partner to the cinema with the two of you now and again. As I said before, third-wheeling isn't inherently bad. You'd be surprised at how enriched you'll feel with that extra

friend in your life, and how much better it is when everyone gets along.

- **Try to understand them.** This part is easier for aros than it is for allos; alloromanticism is everywhere and pretty straightforward in contrast to aromanticism. As I said, however, everyone has their own specific needs, and it's likely that romantic companionship is something your alloromantic friend needs. You may never see the appeal of settling down with anyone, QPP or otherwise, but for a lot of people that aspect of life is very much desired and important. Ask your friend how it feels to be in love, ask them what's so special about it for them; be inquisitive and interested in their life. I have a friend who's interested in football, which I'll never understand, but as a minimum I feel I should ask him when his team is playing, and I'll be pleased for him if his team wins. Watching your friend light up when they talk about something or someone they love should make you feel happy, whether you relate or not. You don't have to share interests with your loved ones; just be interested in them as a person.

I have to admit I have been guilty of this, but please try not to be pleased if your allo friend's relationship doesn't work out. Yes, they'll have more time for you, but remember that this person is grieving and in pain. Understand that just as you'd be heartbroken if you ever lost your friend, they're heartbroken that a relationship dear to them has ended.

- **Have patience.** Sometimes your allo friend will have plans that unfortunately don't involve you. Remember that you're just as important to them as they are to you.

They're not going to forget you exist just because they're all of a sudden engaged and working full-time. If it's been a while since you heard from them, shoot them a text saying you're thinking of them and hope they're okay, just as a reminder that you're there for them.

- **Communicate.** This might seem like an obvious one, but there's no understanding each other without communication. Let your friend know you're scared they'll forget about you, and in turn they'll reassure you that they aren't going anywhere. Listen to your friend when they tell you about the magical date they went on, no matter how romance-repulsed you are. Check in with each other, tell them how proud you are to be part of the aromantic community, but tell them your worries as well.

Ask an aromantic

Whether you're an alloromantic looking to understand more about your aro-spec friend or you're a fully fledged member of the aromantic community giving support to a questioning aromantic, it's important to remember how broad aromanticism is as an orientation. Below are some questions you can ask your aro-spec friend so that you can understand them better or they can better understand themselves:

- Have you ever been in a relationship before? How did it feel? Did it feel forced?
- How do you feel about romance in general? Are you repulsed by it, are you indifferent, or do you feel positively about it? Many aromantic people feel utterly

149

repulsed by the idea or sight of romance, whereas others love the idea. Romantic orientation is purely about who you're attracted to, not what you want.

- Do you feel sexual attraction? What about other kinds of attraction?
- Do you think you've always felt this way but never known the word before, or does it change sometimes?
- Is there any way I can support you?

The main things aro-spec people need are respect and companionship. It's not always easy for people to understand how aros feel, but whether or not you can relate to aromantic people, it's always possible and encouraged to accept them for who they are and how they feel. Verywell Mind put it, um, *very well* in their article 'What it means to be aromantic':

> People understand themselves and their own feelings better than you ever can. Don't dismiss what they feel or insist that they'll change how they feel.[1]

Aros supporting aros

In certain cases, having someone who understands you is the best kind of support. You may have nothing but your romantic orientation in common, but feeling pressured to conform to what other people consider 'normal' or feeling lonely or

1   Cherry, K. (2022) 'What it means to be aromantic.' Verywell Mind. Accessed on 11/11/2022 at www.verywellmind.com/what-does-it-mean-to-be-aromantic-5189571

confused about your identity is something other aro-spec people are more likely to have been through and relate to.

Making connections with other aro-spec people, even if only for support, could be invaluable to you as an aromantic person. You may already have your circle of friends, but it can be difficult and frustrating trying to explain how you feel to someone who's never been there. This is where social media comes in so handy. There are countless subreddits dedicated to aromantic identities, and there are plenty of aro accounts on Twitter and Tumblr – you could even build your own aro support group! Make a website that aro-spec people can go to for moral support, or start a Facebook group where you can all talk about and compare your experiences. Create a community where even if you don't know Tom from Peter, you can all relate to each other and help each other feel at peace.

There's no right or wrong way to build your support network. Whether you confide in your mum or a stranger on the internet, there's always support out there for you.

CHAPTER 8

The Last Bit

Him
I have a question, by the way. I've been doing some reading... Would you consider yourself to be demiromantic/demisexual?

Me
I kinda tweeted a while ago that I'd decided to drop all my labels because... Well, I'm a difficult person to understand, even for myself. I just don't seem to fit into boxes. I've been wondering about the demi thing for a long time, but if I said I was, knowing my luck, it'd change again. I'm not saying my feelings for you would ever change, but I'm kind of sick of changing my labels all the time.

Him
Isn't it possible that you haven't been changing labels as you say, but possibly got the original labels wrong because you weren't aware of the things you're aware

of now? Maybe you're not changing labels; you're just correcting them based on new information.

I've been through many crises like the one above since I started writing this book. As I was finishing up Chapter 6, I was set on introducing this final chapter with a firm proclamation that my label is 'unspecified'. Then I had that conversation with my partner and I felt uncertain all over again.

I've been referring to the aromantic community in the third person throughout this book, unsure if I still fit into it, and doing so has made me nervous. Even just posting on Reddit for contributions to the book, I referred to the aro community in the third person and received these responses:

Are you on the aromantic spectrum yourself?

Wording this as 'their' stories makes it sound like you're not in the aro community yourself, or don't think of yourself to be...

I often say it's entirely your own fault how you react to things, so this is definitely on me, but I read those comments as kind of sceptical and mistrustful. It could be that I projected my own fears of being rejected by those firmly on the aromantic spectrum, but these fears persist whether the comments were meant that way or not.

The term 'WTFromantic' was mentioned in Chapter 2, which is defined as being unsure of your romantic orientation. As I said before, I don't really resonate with the term itself and would definitely just prefer to use 'unspecified'. My partner seems to believe I'm demiromantic, and maybe he's right. Maybe, as he said, all the trying-on of labels was necessary before I arrived at this point.

Thinking back to the mini-quiz in Chapter 2, I could answer many of the questions with certainty: yes, I have a crush on someone. Yes, I would like to kiss, cuddle and have sex with that someone. Yes, I very much desire commitment from him, and yes, I very much want to marry him. Some of my answers would be more complex – how I feel about being single, for example. When I was single, I never craved commitment, I didn't want a relationship, I was happy relying only on myself and I didn't feel like anything was missing. I am extremely happy in my current relationship, however, and therefore do not wish to be single. Does that change how I felt about being single when I was single? Not at all. I wasn't unhappy with being single, so technically I could answer b) I don't mind it. However, in my current mindset I'd be just as inclined to answer d) I prefer having a significant other.

My result: you could be on the aromantic spectrum.

In hindsight, that quiz isn't very helpful at all, but I guess it makes you think!

In Chapter 3, I said this regarding being with my current partner: 'I'm still a bit perplexed as to how or why it happened, or what I am, or if I even belong in the LGBT+ community any more.' I just read that part back, and something dawned on me. Bisexual people feel attracted to more than one gender, and if they ever enter into a relationship with someone of the opposite gender, that doesn't all of a sudden erase their sexuality and make them straight. I've said throughout this book that you can be in a relationship and still be aro-spec, and I don't know why that didn't properly sink in with me *personally*. Maybe my partner is right, and I've been demiromantic all along. Maybe I was right, and I'm still just aroflux.

I'm not going to lie: my label isn't that important to me any more. Labels offer minorities a sense of community, of belonging, and although I'm still unsure who I am in that respect, I feel as though I know where I belong right now. In spite of that, I may never have discovered myself the way I did if it wasn't for the aromantic and asexual communities. Similarly, I like to think I've contributed to the education and visibility of these orientations since discovering them.

My retreat from YouTube and social media in general seems to have given me a different perspective, I think. It's so easy to find that online community and feel so at home in it that when you come out of it and are presented with different outlooks and experiences, sometimes you'll question yourself. I'm not acquainted with any aromantic people in my current situation, and I have one asexual friend whose orientation isn't a huge part of how he presents himself. I feel as if I've gone from immersing myself completely in the aro and ace communities to having no ace or aro connections whatsoever, but it's always been in the back of the mind that yes, I still feel a connection with those orientations. I've never considered myself to be straight, that's for sure. I've never, however, been sexually attracted to women – only romantically. Attraction comes to me in pieces, and a lot of the time I don't know what pieces they are or what to do with them.

The fun thing is, I can decide to pick both labels: aroflux *and* demiromantic – at present, demiromantic feels more or less right, but I've always been fluid in my orientations, so aroflux fits, too. I told my partner I don't like thinking about my orientation any more because it's all so confusing, but I think that's okay. It's okay not to know what your label is, it's okay for labels to change, and it's okay not to use labels at all. I have a lot of appreciation for the people who just go with 'queer'.

In a way, writing this book has really helped me put a lot of coherent thought into my orientation. It's felt a lot like a journal, especially this very self-indulgent final chapter, for which I apologize! But if writing this book has been therapeutic and helpful for me, it gives me hope that it can be a helpful tool for others in my situation. Feeling alien and then realizing you're aromantic is one thing, but still feeling untethered from any particular label and learning to be okay with that is a whole other kind of lonely. I hope if someone feels the way I do, my account here will help them feel a little more at peace with themselves.

I also hope that someone might read this book and find it a little easier to express themselves, feel more hope for their future as an aromantic or understand aromanticism a little bit better.

The aromantics' campaign is only just beginning, but with a world that is becoming increasingly accepting of minorities and all different kinds of people, one day our voices will be heard and not argued with. One day, we'll be more than just four paragraphs at the foot of a Wikipedia page. One day, people will see the aromantic flag and know what it means. Until then, it's not all hopeless.

Be proud of who you are, because no amount of erasure or peer pressure is going to change you.

You're not weird, you're not broken, and you don't have to feel lonely.

You're aromantic, and you don't have to be any other way.

Acknowledgements

It's always been a dream of mine to be a published author, perhaps because I'm so terrible with the spoken word and rather eloquent with the written word, perhaps because I want to be listened to and I want to prove that I'm not as unintelligent as my accent makes me sound! Self-publishing allowed me to somewhat achieve that dream, but this has really taken it to another level, and it couldn't have happened without the support of numerous people.

My sister has read every book I've ever attempted to write, and no matter how terrible it was, she'd always praise it. But at the same time she'd be honest and tell me which parts needed tweaking. She is my biggest supporter and has been a huge help in my growth as a writer.

My parents have always been supportive of my creative endeavours. They believed in me when I said I'd be an author one day, they cheered me on when I attempted to self-publish and they never once told me to get a real job. I suppose it helps that I worked part-time while I was working on my books, but I appreciate their unwavering faith in me all the same.

I don't think I'd have finished this book on time if it weren't for my partner. Admittedly, I'd have been happy spending our days off lounging around, but many times he's forced me out of bed so we could spend a day being productive. Resentful as I was at times, I'm grateful to him for dragging me out into his garden so he could work on his car and supervise my writing. He's cheered me on the whole way, and I really appreciate his support.

Thank you to everyone at JKP, especially Andrew James for offering me the book deal, and Laura Dignum-Smith for continuing to support me after Andrew left to focus on his own creative endeavours.

Thank you to everyone who watched my videos. Without your support, I'd never have been able to write for the *Metro*, and I'd never have been noticed by an *Actual Publisher*. Finishing the book now, it's still hard to believe.

Thank you to everyone who contributed to this book. It honestly wouldn't have been what it is without your contributions and your perspective. An extra thank you to the aromantic people of Twitter – I'm sorry for all the questions I hurled at you over the last year, but thank you for taking the time to answer them.

Thank you to the aromantic community. Although somehow I managed to find love, I still would've spent a massive chunk of my life questioning what the hell was wrong with me up until then if you didn't exist. Thank you for allowing me to explore myself. Thank you for accepting me as one of your own.

And finally, thank you to you, the reader. Thank you for giving aromanticism your attention. Thank you for being here to witness my crisis!

All my love,

Sammy x

Glossary

This section includes terms used multiple times throughout the book for any casual or forgetful readers. Any terms only used once and defined in that instance will not be repeated on this page.

A communities	refers to the aromantic, asexual and agender communities as a whole.
Ace	abbreviation for asexual, informal.
Aesthetic attraction	liking the way someone looks, finding them attractive to the eye.
Allo	someone who feels attraction. Alloromantic people feel romantic attraction, allosexual people feel sexual attraction, and so on.
Ally	someone outside of the LGBT+ community who fully supports and advocates for its members.
Amatonormativity	the normalization of traditional romantic/sexual relationships.
Aro	abbreviation for aromantic.

Aro-spec	abbreviation for aromantic spectrum.
Aroflux	one who fluctuates on the aromantic spectrum.
Cisgender	identifies with the gender assigned at birth.
Cishet	abbreviation for cisgender heterosexual.
Cupioromantic	someone who wants to be in a romantic relationship but lacks romantic attraction.
Demiromantic	one who feels romantic attraction under very specific circumstances, or when a close bond has been formed.
Heteronormative	the normalization of a heteroromanticism/heterosexuality.
LGBT+	abbreviation for LGBTQIA, which stands for lesbian, gay, transgender, queer, intersex and aromantic/asexual/agender.
Lithromantic	one who feels romantic attraction until it's reciprocated.
Minority	a small group of people, fewer than the majority.
Misconception	a falsehood believed to be true.
Panromantic	someone who is romantically attracted to people regardless of gender.
Pansexual	someone who is sexually attracted to people regardless of gender.
Platonic	in a friendly manner.
Polyamory	being in multiple relationships at once, usually with the consent of all parties.
Queerplatonic	a special, close bond that isn't inherently romantic or sexual, but is more exclusive than traditional friendship.

QPP/QPR	abbreviations for queerplatonic partner or queerplatonic relationship.
Quoiromantic	refers to someone who cannot wrap their head around the idea of romance.
Recipromantic	one who can only feel romantic attraction if they know the other person feels the same.
Spectrum	a broad scale.

Influencers, Sources and Helplines

Aromantic content

Below is a list as comprehensive as I could make of aromantic influencers. Some of the people on this list may not be aromantic themselves, but they provide information on aromanticism on their platforms.

- **Yasmin Benoit**
  - Model, aromantic asexual activist, and occasional YouTuber.
  - YouTube: www.youtube.com/c/YasminBenoit
  - Twitter and Instagram: @theyasminbenoit
- **Celeste M**
  - Trans aromantic asexual YouTuber. Posts mostly about their gender, but their backlog contains a few videos on aromanticism.
  - YouTube: www.youtube.com/c/CelesteM

- **Slice of Ace**
  - Homoromantic asexual YouTuber who also makes videos on romantic orientation from time to time.
  - YouTube: www.youtube.com/c/SliceofAce
  - Twitter: @sliceoface
- **Lynn Saga**
  - Bi/ace YouTuber who also makes videos on aromanticism.
  - YouTube: www.youtube.com/channel/UCX7NS4P5Ms-OV4RLg7x8gTw/featured
  - Twitter: @lynnsaga
  - Instagram: @lynnsaga01
- **Samantha Aimee**
  - Um, that's me. Hi.
  - YouTube: www.youtube.com/c/SamanthaAimee
  - Twitter: @sammyaimeee
  - Instagram: @samantha.aimeee
- **Kya**
  - Host of the DissociaDID system. DissociaDID mostly post YouTube videos about mental health, but Kya has recently come out as aroace which is huge for the A communities as DissociaDID has a whopping 1.18 *million* subscribers!
  - YouTube: www.youtube.com/channel/UC6kFD5xIFvWyLlytv5pTR1w
  - Instagram: @dissociadid
- **Spacey Aces**
  - A YouTube channel run by three aro- and/or ace-spec people which features videos about sexual and romantic orientation.
  - YouTube: www.youtube.com/c/SpaceyAces

Other YouTube videos I can recommend:

- I spent a day with ROMANCE REPULSED ARO-MANTICS by Anthony Padilla: www.youtube.com/watch?v=Giscu5wuC_U
- Aromantic Spectrum Identities (Aro-Spec) | Under The Queer Umbrella by Under the Umbrellas with Jay-jay: www.youtube.com/watch?v=BpIklDoIldw&t=656s
- What falls under the Aromantic Spectrum? | Under the Rainbow by Queer 2 Help: www.youtube.com/watch?v=clKYs7OuNuk

Other sources

Below are some sites on aromanticism you may find helpful:

- **AUREA** (Aromantic-spectrum Union for Recognition, Education, and Advocacy): www.aromanticism.org
- **LGBTQIA+ Wiki** (a website dedicated to educating on all LGBT+ identities): https://lgbtqia.fandom.com/wiki/LGBTQIA%2B_Wiki
- **Sounds Fake But Okay** (a podcast by two ace-/aro-spec people about asexuality and aromanticism): www.soundsfakepod.com
- **Aromantic-official** (a tumblr blog dedicated to helping aro-spec people and educating on aromanticism): https://aromantic-official.tumblr.com
- **r/aromantic** (the Reddit page for aromanticism): www.reddit.com/r/aromantic

LGBT+ helplines

A few helplines were mentioned in Chapter 6, but most were UK-exclusive so I'll list a few international ones here. If you feel you need help, please reach out.

- LGBT National Help Center (USA): www.lgbthotline.org
- National Suicide Prevention Lifeline (USA): 1-800-273-8255
- LGBT Youthline (Canada): 1-800-268-9688
- Lifeline (Australia): 13 11 14
- Outline (New Zealand): 0800 688 5463
- LGBT Helpline (Ireland): 1890 929 539

Index